The Misanthrope AND *Tartuffe*

BY RICHARD WILBUR

The Beautiful Changes and Other Poems

Ceremony and Other Poems

A Bestiary
(editor, with Alexander Calder)

Molière's *The Misanthrope*
(translator)

Things of This World
(poems)

Poems 1943-1956

Candide
(comic opera, with Lillian Hellman)

Poe: Complete Poems
(editor)

Advice to a Prophet and Other Poems

Molière's *Tartuffe*
(translator)

The Poems of Richard Wilbur

Loudmouse
(for children)

Shakespeare: Poems
(co-editor, with Alfred Harbage)

Walking to Sleep: New Poems and Translations

Molière's *The School for Wives*
(translator)

Opposites
(for children)

The Mind-Reader: New Poems

Responses: Prose Pieces: 1953-1976

Molières *The Learned Ladies*
(translator)

JEAN BAPTISTE POQUELIN DE MOLIÈRE

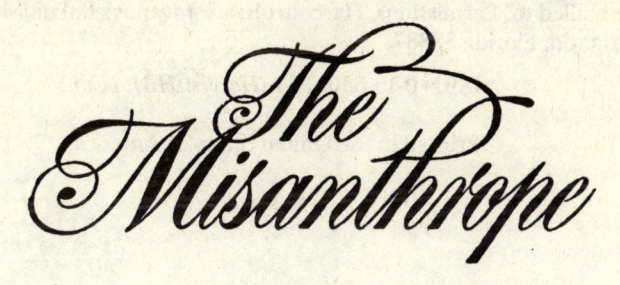

The Misanthrope

AND

Tartuffe

TRANSLATED INTO ENGLISH VERSE BY
RICHARD WILBUR

Drawings by Enrico Arno

HBJ

A Harvest/HBJ Book
Harcourt Brace Jovanovich, Publishers
San Diego   New York   London

Copyright © 1954, 1955, 1961, 1962, 1963, 1965 by Richard Wilbur

All rights reserved. No part of this publication may be reproduced or transmitted in any form or by any means, electronic or mechanical, including photocopy, recording, or any information storage and retrieval system, without permission in writing from the publisher.

Requests for permission to make copies of any part of the work should be mailed to: Permissions, Harcourt Brace Jovanovich, Publishers, Orlando, Florida 32887.

ISBN 0-15-660517-1 *(Harvest/HBJ: pbk.)*

Printed in the United States of America

W X Y Z

CAUTION: Professionals and amateurs are hereby warned that these translations, being fully protected under the copyright laws of the United States of America, the British Empire, including the Dominion of Canada, and all other countries which are signatories to the Universal Copyright Convention and the International Copyright Union, is subject to royalty. All rights, including professional, amateur, motion picture, recitation, lecturing, public reading, radio broadcasting, and television, are strictly reserved. Particular emphasis is laid on the question of readings, permission for which must be secured from the author's agent in writing. Inquiries on professional rights (except for amateur rights) should be addressed to Mr. Gilbert Parker, Curtis Brown, Ltd., 60 East 56 Street, New York, New York 10022; inquiries on translation rights should be addressed to Harcourt Brace Jovanovich, Publishers, Orlando, FL 32887.

The amateur acting rights of Tartuffe are controlled exclusively by the Dramatists Play Service, Inc., 440 Park Avenue South, New York, New York. No amateur performance of the play may be given without obtaining in advance the written permission of the Dramatists Play Service, Inc., and paying the requisite fee.

Act One, Scene Two, of this translation of *The Misanthrope* was first published in *New World Writing 5*. Certain scenes of this translation of *Tartuffe* appeared in *Poetry*, *Drama Critique*, and the *Massachusetts Review*.

A Note to the Harvest Edition

There are one or two things I should like to say to those who will be using this edition of *The Misanthrope* and *Tartuffe* as a script. These translations have had the good luck to be performed, a number of times, in New York, regional, and university theaters, and also on radio and on television. The best of the stage productions have repeatedly proved what the fact of radio production would suggest: the verbal sufficiency of Molière's serious comedies. What the plays are about, what the characters think, feel, and do, is clearly and amply presented in the dialogue, so that a mere reading-aloud of the lines, without any effort at performance, can provide a complete, if austere, experience of the work.

I do not mean to say that there are no open questions in either play. To what extent do Philinte and Cléante, in their reasonable yet ineffectual speeches, express the playwright's view of things? Is Célimène incorrigibly trivial, or is she in process of developing a moral sensitivity, a capacity for love? Is it possible that Tartuffe possesses, in his real and underlying nature, a kind of balked religious yearning? And what on earth does Elmire see in Orgon? These are questions that director and actor may, and indeed must, decide; but it will be found that Molière's comedy, because it is so thoroughly "written," resists the overextension of any thesis. The actor or director who insists on a stimulatingly freakish interpretation will find himself engaged in deliberate misreading and willful distortion, and the audience will not be deceived.

In short, trust the words. Trust the words to convey the point and persons of the comedy, and trust them also to be

[*A Note to the Harvest Edition*]

sufficiently entertaining. A fussy anxiety on the part of the director, whereby the dialogue is hurried, cut, or swamped in farcical action, is the commonest cause of failure in productions of Molière. To such want of confidence in the text we owe the occasional presentation of the fops, Acaste and Clitandre, as flouncingly epicene, or the transformation of Tartuffe's two interviews with Elmire into a couple of wrestling bouts. In the first case the characters are falsified for the sake of an easy laugh, and cease to be legitimate rivals to Alceste for the hand of Célimène; in the second case, a real quality of Tartuffe's—his lustfulness—is manifested, but at the cost of making his great speeches seem redundant and pointlessly nuanced. The cost is too great, and once again the audience, though it may consent to laugh, will not be satisfied.

The introductions to the original editions still say what I think, and I shall let them stand. Were I to revise them, the second would explicitly and gratefully refer to the criticism of Jacques Guicharnaud, and each would contain a qualification of my claim to accuracy. The translation of *The Misanthrope* does not fully reproduce the formulaic preciosity with which some of the characters speak of love. In translating *Tartuffe*, I have not always captured Madame Pernelle's way of slipping into old-fashioned and inelegant speech, or Mariane's of parroting the rhetoric of artificial romances. My excuse for these deficiencies is that, while echoes of an unchanging scripture or liturgy are readily duplicated, as in the speeches of Tartuffe, a translation that seeks to avoid a "period" diction cannot easily find equivalents for such quirks and fads of language as I have mentioned.

R. W.

Portland, Connecticut, 1965

THE MISANTHROPE

The Misanthrope

COMEDY IN FIVE ACTS, 1666

To Harry Levin

INTRODUCTION

The idea that comedy is a ritual in which society's laughter corrects individual extravagance is particularly inapplicable to *The Misanthrope*. In this play, society itself is indicted, and though Alceste's criticisms are indiscriminate, they are not unjustified. It is true that falseness and intrigue are everywhere on view; the conventions enforce a routine dishonesty, justice is subverted by influence, love is overwhelmed by calculation, and these things are accepted, even by the best, as "natural." The cold vanity of Oronte, Acaste, and Clitandre, the malignant hypocrisy of Arsinoé, the insincerity of Célimène, are to be taken as exemplary of the age, and Philinte's philosophic tolerance will not quite do in response to such a condition of things. The honest Éliante is the one we are most to trust, and this is partly because she sees that Alceste's intransigence *A quelque chose en soy de noble & d'héroïque*.

But *The Misanthrope* is not only a critique of society; it is also a study of impurity of motive in a critic of society. If Alceste has a rage for the genuine, and he truly has, it is unfortunately compromised and exploited by his vast, unconscious egotism. He is a jealous friend (*Je veux qu'on me distingue*), and it is Philinte's polite effusiveness toward another which prompts his attack on promiscuous civility. He is a jealous lover, and his "frankness" about Oronte's sonnet owes something to the fact that Oronte is his rival, and that the sonnet is addressed to Célimène. Like many humorless and indignant people, he is hard on everybody but himself, and does not perceive it when he fails his own ideal. In one aspect, Alceste seems a moral giant misplaced in a trivial society, having (in George Eliot's phrase) "a

[*Introduction*]

certain spiritual grandeur ill-matched with the meanness of opportunity"; in another aspect, he seems an unconscious fraud who magnifies the petty faults of others in order to dramatize himself in his own eyes.

He is, of course, both at once: but the two impressions predominate by turns. A victim, like all around him, of the moral enervation of the times, he cannot consistently be the Man of Honor—simple, magnanimous, passionate, decisive, true. It is his distinction that he is aware of that ideal, and that he can fitfully embody it; his comic flaw consists in a Quixotic confusion of himself with the ideal, a willingness to distort the world for his own self-deceptive and histrionic purposes. Paradoxically, then, the advocate of true feeling and honest intercourse is the one character most artificial, most out-of-touch, most in danger of that nonentity and solitude which all, in the chattery, hollow world of this play, are fleeing. He must play-act continually in order to believe in his own existence, and he welcomes the fact or show of injustice as a dramatic cue. At the close of the play, when Alceste has refused to appeal his lawsuit and has spurned the hand of Célimène, one cannot escape the suspicion that his indignation is in great part instrumental, a desperate means of counterfeiting an identity.

Martin Turnell (whose book *The Classical Moment* contains a fine analysis of *The Misanthrope*) observes that those speeches of Alceste which ring most false are, as it were, parodies of "Cornelian *tirade*." To duplicate this parody-tragic effect in English it was clearly necessary to keep the play in verse, where it would be possible to control the tone more sharply, and to recall our own tragic tradition. There were other reasons, too, for approximating Molière's form. The constant of rhythm and rhyme was needed, in the translation as in the original, for bridging great gaps between high comedy and farce, lofty diction and ordinary talk, deep character and shallow. Again, while prose might preserve the thematic structure of the play, other "musical" elements would be lost, in particular the frequently intricate arrangements of balancing half-lines, lines, couplets, quatrains, and sestets. There is no question that words, when dancing within such patterns, are not their prosaic selves, but have a wholly different mood and meaning.

Consider, finally, two peculiarities of the dialogue of the play: redundancy and logic. When Molière has a character repeat essentially the same thing in three successive couplets, it will sometimes have a very clear dramatic point; but it will always have the intention of stabilizing the idea against the movement of the verse, and of giving a specifically rhetorical pleasure. In a prose rendering, these latter effects are lost, and the passage tends to seem merely prolix. As for logic, it is a convention of *The Misanthrope* that its main characters can express themselves logically, and in the most complex grammar; Molière's dramatic verse, which is almost wholly free of metaphor, derives much of its richness from argumentative virtuosity. Here is a bit of logic from Arsinoé:

> *Madame, l'Amitié doit sur tout éclater*
> *Aux choses qui le plus nous peuvent importer:*
> *Et comme il n'en est point de plus grande importance*
> *Que celles de l'Honneur et de la Bienséance,*
> *Je viens par un avis qui touche vostre honneur*
> *Témoigner l'amitié que pour vous a mon Coeur.*

In prose it might come out like this: "Madam, friendship should most display itself when truly vital matters are in question: and since there are no things more vital than decency and honor, I have come to prove my heartfelt friendship by giving you some advice which concerns your reputation." Even if that were better rendered, it would still be plain that Molière's logic loses all its baroque exuberance in prose; it sounds lawyerish; without rhyme and verse

[*Introduction*]

to phrase and emphasize the steps of its progression, the logic becomes obscure like Congreve's, not crystalline and followable as it was meant to be.

For all these reasons, rhymed verse seemed to me obligatory. The choice did not preclude accuracy, and what follows is, I believe, a line-for-line verse translation quite as faithful as any which have been done in prose. I hasten to say that I am boasting only of patience; a translation may, alas, be faithful on all counts, and still lack quality.

One word about diction. This is a play in which French aristocrats of 1666 converse about their special concerns, and employ the moral and philosophical terms peculiar to their thought. Not all my words, therefore, are strictly modern; I had for example to use "spleen" and "phlegm"; but I think that I have avoided the zounds sort of thing, and that at best the diction mediates between then and now, suggesting no one period. There are occasional vulgarities, but for these there is precedent in the original, Molière's people being aristocrats and therefore not genteel.

If this English version is played or read aloud, the names should be pronounced in a fashion *roughly* French, without nasal and uvular agonies. Damon should be *dah-MOAN*, and for rhythmic convenience Arsinoé should be *ar-SIN-oh-eh*.

My translation was begun in late 1952 in New Mexico, during a fellowship from the Guggenheim Foundation, and finished this year in Rome under grants from the American Academy of Arts & Letters and the Chapelbrook Foundation. To these organizations, and to certain individuals who have befriended the project, I am very grateful.

R. W.

Wellesley, Massachusetts.

CHARACTERS

ALCESTE, in love with Célimène
PHILINTE, Alceste's friend
ORONTE, in love with Célimène
CELIMENE, Alceste's beloved
ELIANTE, Célimène's cousin
ARSINOE, a friend of Célimène's
ACASTE ⎫
        ⎬ marquesses
CLITANDRE ⎭
BASQUE, Célimène's servant
A GUARD of the Marshalsea
DUBOIS, Alceste's valet

The scene throughout is in Célimène's house at Paris.

First produced by The Poets' Theatre, *Cambridge, on October 25th, 1955*

Act 1

SCENE ONE

PHILINTE, ALCESTE

PHILINTE

Now, what's got into you?

ALCESTE, *seated*

Kindly leave me alone.

PHILINTE

Come, come, what is it? This lugubrious tone . . .

ALCESTE

Leave me, I said; you spoil my solitude.

PHILINTE

Oh, listen to me, now, and don't be rude.

ALCESTE

I choose to be rude, Sir, and to be hard of hearing.

[Act One · Scene One]

PHILINTE

These ugly moods of yours are not endearing;
Friends though we are, I really must insist . . .

ALCESTE, *abruptly rising*

Friends? Friends, you say? Well, cross me off your list.
I've been your friend till now, as you well know;
But after what I saw a moment ago
I tell you flatly that our ways must part.
I wish no place in a dishonest heart.

PHILINTE

Why, what have I done, Alceste? Is this quite just?

ALCESTE

My God, you ought to die of self-disgust.
I call your conduct inexcusable, Sir,
And every man of honor will concur.
I see you almost hug a man to death,
Exclaim for joy until you're out of breath,
And supplement these loving demonstrations
With endless offers, vows, and protestations;
Then when I ask you "Who was that?", I find
That you can barely bring his name to mind!
Once the man's back is turned, you cease to love him,
And speak with absolute indifference of him!
By God, I say it's base and scandalous
To falsify the heart's affections thus;

[*Act One · Scene One*]

If I caught myself behaving in such a way,
I'd hang myself for shame, without delay.

PHILINTE

It hardly seems a hanging matter to me;
I hope that you will take it graciously
If I extend myself a slight reprieve,
And live a little longer, by your leave.

ALCESTE

How dare you joke about a crime so grave?

PHILINTE

What crime? How else are people to behave?

ALCESTE

I'd have them be sincere, and never part
With any word that isn't from the heart.

PHILINTE

When someone greets us with a show of pleasure,
It's but polite to give him equal measure,
Return his love the best that we know how,
And trade him offer for offer, vow for vow.

ALCESTE

No, no, this formula you'd have me follow,
However fashionable, is false and hollow,

[*Act One · Scene One*]

And I despise the frenzied operations
Of all these barterers of protestations,
These lavishers of meaningless embraces,
These utterers of obliging commonplaces,
Who court and flatter everyone on earth
And praise the fool no less than the man of worth.
Should you rejoice that someone fondles you,
Offers his love and service, swears to be true,
And fills your ears with praises of your name,
When to the first damned fop he'll say the same?
No, no: no self-respecting heart would dream
Of prizing so promiscuous an esteem;
However high the praise, there's nothing worse
Than sharing honors with the universe.
Esteem is founded on comparison:
To honor all men is to honor none.
Since you embrace this indiscriminate vice,
Your friendship comes at far too cheap a price;
I spurn the easy tribute of a heart
Which will not set the worthy man apart:
I choose, Sir, to be chosen; and in fine,
The friend of mankind is no friend of mine.

PHILINTE

But in polite society, custom decrees
That we show certain outward courtesies. . . .

ALCESTE

Ah, no! we should condemn with all our force
Such false and artificial intercourse.
Let men behave like men; let them display

[Act One · Scene One]

Their inmost hearts in everything they say;
Let the heart speak, and let our sentiments
Not mask themselves in silly compliments.

PHILINTE

In certain cases it would be uncouth
And most absurd to speak the naked truth;
With all respect for your exalted notions,
It's often best to veil one's true emotions.
Wouldn't the social fabric come undone
If we were wholly frank with everyone?
Suppose you met with someone you couldn't bear;
Would you inform him of it then and there?

ALCESTE

Yes.

PHILINTE

Then you'd tell old Émilie it's pathetic
The way she daubs her features with cosmetic
And plays the gay coquette at sixty-four?

ALCESTE

I would.

PHILINTE

And you'd call Dorilas a bore,
And tell him every ear at court is lame
From hearing him brag about his noble name?

[Act One · Scene One]

ALCESTE

Precisely.

PHILINTE

Ah, you're joking.

ALCESTE

Au contraire:
In this regard there's none I'd choose to spare.
All are corrupt; there's nothing to be seen
In court or town but aggravates my spleen.
I fall into deep gloom and melancholy
When I survey the scene of human folly,
Finding on every hand base flattery,
Injustice, fraud, self-interest, treachery. . . .
Ah, it's too much; mankind has grown so base,
I mean to break with the whole human race.

PHILINTE

This philosophic rage is a bit extreme;
You've no idea how comical you seem;
Indeed, we're like those brothers in the play
Called *School for Husbands*, one of whom was prey . . .

ALCESTE

Enough, now! None of your stupid similes.

[*Act One · Scene One*]

PHILINTE

Then let's have no more tirades, if you please.
The world won't change, whatever you say or do;
And since plain speaking means so much to you,
I'll tell you plainly that by being frank
You've earned the reputation of a crank,
And that you're thought ridiculous when you rage
And rant against the manners of the age.

ALCESTE

So much the better; just what I wish to hear.
No news could be more grateful to my ear.
All men are so detestable in my eyes,
I should be sorry if they thought me wise.

PHILINTE

Your hatred's very sweeping, is it not?

ALCESTE

Quite right: I hate the whole degraded lot.

PHILINTE

Must all poor human creatures be embraced,
Without distinction, by your vast distaste?
Even in these bad times, there are surely a few . . .

[Act One · Scene One]

ALCESTE

No, I include all men in one dim view:
Some men I hate for being rogues; the others
I hate because they treat the rogues like brothers,
And, lacking a virtuous scorn for what is vile,
Receive the villain with a complaisant smile.
Notice how tolerant people choose to be
Toward that bold rascal who's at law with me.
His social polish can't conceal his nature;
One sees at once that he's a treacherous creature;
No one could possibly be taken in
By those soft speeches and that sugary grin.
The whole world knows the shady means by which
The low-brow's grown so powerful and rich,
And risen to a rank so bright and high
That virtue can but blush, and merit sigh.
Whenever his name comes up in conversation,
None will defend his wretched reputation;
Call him knave, liar, scoundrel, and all the rest,
Each head will nod, and no one will protest.
And yet his smirk is seen in every house,
He's greeted everywhere with smiles and bows,
And when there's any honor that can be got
By pulling strings, he'll get it, like as not.
My God! It chills my heart to see the ways
Men come to terms with evil nowadays;
Sometimes, I swear, I'm moved to flee and find
Some desert land unfouled by humankind.

[Act One · Scene One]

PHILINTE

Come, let's forget the follies of the times
And pardon mankind for its petty crimes;
Let's have an end of rantings and of railings,
And show some leniency toward human failings.
This world requires a pliant rectitude;
Too stern a virtue makes one stiff and rude;
Good sense views all extremes with detestation,
And bids us to be noble in moderation.
The rigid virtues of the ancient days
Are not for us; they jar with all our ways
And ask of us too lofty a perfection.
Wise men accept their times without objection,
And there's no greater folly, if you ask me,
Than trying to reform society.
Like you, I see each day a hundred and one
Unhandsome deeds that might be better done,
But still, for all the faults that meet my view,
I'm never known to storm and rave like you.
I take men as they are, or let them be,
And teach my soul to bear their frailty;
And whether in court or town, whatever the scene,
My phlegm's as philosophic as your spleen.

ALCESTE

This phlegm which you so eloquently commend,
Does nothing ever rile it up, my friend?
Suppose some man you trust should treacherously
Conspire to rob you of your property,
And do his best to wreck your reputation?
Wouldn't you feel a certain indignation?

[*Act One · Scene One*]

PHILINTE

Why, no. These faults of which you so complain
Are part of human nature, I maintain,
And it's no more a matter for disgust
That men are knavish, selfish and unjust,
Than that the vulture dines upon the dead,
And wolves are furious, and apes ill-bred.

ALCESTE

Shall I see myself betrayed, robbed, torn to bits,
And not . . . Oh, let's be still and rest our wits.
Enough of reasoning, now. I've had my fill.

PHILINTE

Indeed, you would do well, Sir, to be still.
Rage less at your opponent, and give some thought
To how you'll win this lawsuit that he's brought.

ALCESTE

I assure you I'll do nothing of the sort.

PHILINTE

Then who will plead your case before the court?

ALCESTE

Reason and right and justice will plead for me.

[*Act One* · *Scene One*]

PHILINTE

Oh, Lord. What judges do you plan to see?

ALCESTE

Why, none. The justice of my cause is clear.

PHILINTE

Of course, man; but there's politics to fear. . . .

ALCESTE

No, I refuse to lift a hand. That's flat.
I'm either right, or wrong.

PHILINTE

          Don't count on that.

ALCESTE

No, I'll do nothing.

PHILINTE

          Your enemy's influence
Is great, you know . . .

ALCESTE

          That makes no difference.

[*Act One · Scene One*]

PHILINTE

It will; you'll see.

ALCESTE

Must honor bow to guile?
If so, I shall be proud to lose the trial.

PHILINTE

Oh, really . . .

ALCESTE

I'll discover by this case
Whether or not men are sufficiently base
And impudent and villainous and perverse
To do me wrong before the universe.

PHILINTE

What a man!

ALCESTE

Oh, I could wish, whatever the cost,
Just for the beauty of it, that my trial were lost.

PHILINTE

If people heard you talking so, Alceste,
They'd split their sides. Your name would be a jest.

[Act One · Scene One]

ALCESTE

So much the worse for jesters.

PHILINTE

                    May I enquire
Whether this rectitude you so admire,
And these hard virtues you're enamored of
Are qualities of the lady whom you love?
It much surprises me that you, who seem
To view mankind with furious disesteem,
Have yet found something to enchant your eyes
Amidst a species which you so despise.
And what is more amazing, I'm afraid,
Is the most curious choice your heart has made.
The honest Eliante is fond of you,
Arsinoé, the prude, admires you too;
And yet your spirit's been perversely led
To choose the flighty Célimène instead,
Whose brittle malice and coquettish ways
So typify the manners of our days.
How is it that the traits you most abhor
Are bearable in this lady you adore?
Are you so blind with love that you can't find them?
Or do you contrive, in her case, not to mind them?

ALCESTE

My love for that young widow's not the kind
That can't perceive defects; no, I'm not blind.
I see her faults, despite my ardent love,

[*Act One · Scene One*]

And all I see I fervently reprove.
And yet I'm weak; for all her falsity,
That woman knows the art of pleasing me,
And though I never cease complaining of her,
I swear I cannot manage not to love her.
Her charm outweighs her faults; I can but aim
To cleanse her spirit in my love's pure flame.

PHILINTE

That's no small task; I wish you all success.
You think then that she loves you?

ALCESTE

                    Heavens, yes!
I wouldn't love her did she not love me.

PHILINTE

Well, if her taste for you is plain to see,
Why do these rivals cause you such despair?

ALCESTE

True love, Sir, is possessive, and cannot bear
To share with all the world. I'm here today
To tell her she must send that mob away.

PHILINTE

If I were you, and had your choice to make,
Eliante, her cousin, would be the one I'd take;

[*Act One · Scene One*]

That honest heart, which cares for you alone,
Would harmonize far better with your own.

ALCESTE

True, true: each day my reason tells me so;
But reason doesn't rule in love, you know.

PHILINTE

I fear some bitter sorrow is in store;
This love . . .

SCENE TWO

ORONTE, ALCESTE, PHILINTE

ORONTE, *to Alceste*

The servants told me at the door
That Eliante and Célimène were out,
But when I heard, dear Sir, that you were about,
I came to say, without exaggeration,
That I hold you in the vastest admiration,
And that it's always been my dearest desire
To be the friend of one I so admire.
I hope to see my love of merit requited,
And you and me in friendship's bond united.
I'm sure you won't refuse—if I may be frank—
A friend of my devotedness—and rank.
   (*During this speech of Oronte's, Alceste is abstracted, and seems unaware that he is being spoken to. He only breaks off his reverie when Oronte says:*)
It was for you, if you please, that my words were intended.

ALCESTE

For me, Sir?

[*Act One · Scene Two*]

ORONTE

Yes, for you. You're not offended?

ALCESTE

By no means. But this much surprises me. . . .
The honor comes most unexpectedly. . . .

ORONTE

My high regard should not astonish you;
The whole world feels the same. It is your due.

ALCESTE

Sir . . .

ORONTE

Why, in all the State there isn't one
Can match your merits; they shine, Sir, like the sun.

ALCESTE

Sir . . .

ORONTE

You are higher in my estimation
Than all that's most illustrious in the nation.

[Act One · Scene Two]

ALCESTE

Sir . . .

ORONTE

If I lie, may heaven strike me dead!
To show you that I mean what I have said,
Permit me, Sir, to embrace you most sincerely,
And swear that I will prize our friendship dearly.
Give me your hand. And now, Sir, if you choose,
We'll make our vows.

ALCESTE

Sir . . .

ORONTE

What! You refuse?

ALCESTE

Sir, it's a very great honor you extend:
But friendship is a sacred thing, my friend;
It would be profanation to bestow
The name of friend on one you hardly know.
All parts are better played when well-rehearsed;
Let's put off friendship, and get acquainted first.
We may discover it would be unwise
To try to make our natures harmonize.

[Act One · Scene Two]

ORONTE

By heaven! You're sagacious to the core;
This speech has made me admire you even more.
Let time, then, bring us closer day by day;
Meanwhile, I shall be yours in every way.
If, for example, there should be anything
You wish at court, I'll mention it to the King.
I have his ear, of course; it's quite well known
That I am much in favor with the throne.
In short, I am your servant. And now, dear friend,
Since you have such fine judgment, I intend
To please you, if I can, with a small sonnet
I wrote not long ago. Please comment on it,
And tell me whether I ought to publish it.

ALCESTE

You must excuse me, Sir; I'm hardly fit
To judge such matters.

ORONTE

Why not?

ALCESTE

      I am, I fear,
Inclined to be unfashionably sincere.

[*Act One · Scene Two*]

ORONTE

Just what I ask; I'd take no satisfaction
In anything but your sincere reaction.
I beg you not to dream of being kind.

ALCESTE

Since you desire it, Sir, I'll speak my mind.

ORONTE

Sonnet. It's a sonnet. . . . *Hope* . . . The poem's addressed
To a lady who wakened hopes within my breast.
Hope . . . this is not the pompous sort of thing,
Just modest little verses, with a tender ring.

ALCESTE

Well, we shall see.

ORONTE

Hope . . . I'm anxious to hear
Whether the style seems properly smooth and clear,
And whether the choice of words is good or bad.

ALCESTE

We'll see, we'll see.

[Act One · Scene Two]

ORONTE

      Perhaps I ought to add
That it took me only a quarter-hour to write it.

ALCESTE

The time's irrelevant, Sir: kindly recite it.

ORONTE, *reading*

Hope comforts us awhile, t'is true,
Lulling our cares with careless laughter,
And yet such joy is full of rue,
My Phyllis, if nothing follows after.

PHILINTE

I'm charmed by this already; the style's delightful.

ALCESTE, *sotto voce, to Philinte*

How can you say that? Why, the thing is frightful.

ORONTE

Your fair face smiled on me awhile,
But was it kindness so to enchant me?
'Twould have been fairer not to smile,
If hope was all you meant to grant me.

[*Act One · Scene Two*]

PHILINTE

What a clever thought! How handsomely you phrase it!

ALCESTE, *sotto voce, to Philinte*

You know the thing is trash. How dare you praise it?

ORONTE

If it's to be my passion's fate
Thus everlastingly to wait,
Then death will come to set me free:
For death is fairer than the fair;
Phyllis, to hope is to despair
When one must hope eternally.

PHILINTE

The close is exquisite—full of feeling and grace.

ALCESTE, *sotto voce, aside*

Oh, blast the close; you'd better close your face
Before you send your lying soul to hell.

PHILINTE

I can't remember a poem I've liked so well.

[Act One · Scene Two]

ALCESTE, *sotto voce, aside*

Good Lord!

ORONTE, *to Philinte*

I fear you're flattering me a bit.

PHILINTE

Oh, no!

ALCESTE, *sotto voce, aside*

What else d'you call it, you hypocrite?

ORONTE, *to Alceste*

But you, Sir, keep your promise now: don't shrink
From telling me sincerely what you think.

ALCESTE

Sir, these are delicate matters; we all desire
To be told that we've the true poetic fire.
But once, to one whose name I shall not mention,
I said, regarding some verse of his invention,
That gentlemen should rigorously control
That itch to write which often afflicts the soul;
That one should curb the heady inclination
To publicize one's little avocation;
And that in showing off one's works of art
One often plays a very clownish part.

[*Act One · Scene Two*]

ORONTE

Are you suggesting in a devious way
That I ought not . . .

ALCESTE

                Oh, that I do not say.
Further, I told him that no fault is worse
Than that of writing frigid, lifeless verse,
And that the merest whisper of such a shame
Suffices to destroy a man's good name.

ORONTE

D'you mean to say my sonnet's dull and trite?

ALCESTE

I don't say that. But I went on to cite
Numerous cases of once-respected men
Who came to grief by taking up the pen.

ORONTE

And am I like them? Do I write so poorly?

ALCESTE

I don't say that. But I told this person, "Surely
You're under no necessity to compose;
Why you should wish to publish, heaven knows.

[*Act One · Scene Two*]

There's no excuse for printing tedious rot
Unless one writes for bread, as you do not.
Resist temptation, then, I beg of you;
Conceal your pastimes from the public view;
And don't give up, on any provocation,
Your present high and courtly reputation,
To purchase at a greedy printer's shop
The name of silly author and scribbling fop."
These were the points I tried to make him see.

ORONTE

I sense that they are also aimed at me;
But now—about my sonnet—I'd like to be told . . .

ALCESTE

Frankly, that sonnet should be pigeonholed.
You've chosen the worst models to imitate.
The style's unnatural. Let me illustrate:

> For example, *Your fair face smiled on me awhile,*
> Followed by, *'Twould have been fairer not to smile!*
> Or this: *such joy is full of rue;*
> Or this: *For death is fairer than the fair;*
> Or, *Phyllis, to hope is to despair*
>   *When one must hope eternally!*

This artificial style, that's all the fashion,
Has neither taste, nor honesty, nor passion;
It's nothing but a sort of wordy play,
And nature never spoke in such a way.
What, in this shallow age, is not debased?
Our fathers, though less refined, had better taste;

[*Act One · Scene Two*]

I'd barter all that men admire today
For one old love-song I shall try to say:

> *If the King had given me for my own*
> *Paris, his citadel,*
> *And I for that must leave alone*
> *Her whom I love so well,*
> *I'd say then to the Crown,*
> *Take back your glittering town;*
> *My darling is more fair, I swear,*
> *My darling is more fair.*

The rhyme's not rich, the style is rough and old,
But don't you see that it's the purest gold
Beside the tinsel nonsense now preferred,
And that there's passion in its every word?

> *If the King had given me for my own*
> *Paris, his citadel,*
> *And I for that must leave alone*
> *Her whom I love so well,*
> *I'd say then to the Crown,*
> *Take back your glittering town;*
> *My darling is more fair, I swear,*
> *My darling is more fair.*

There speaks a loving heart. (*To Philinte*) You're laughing, eh?
Laugh on, my precious wit. Whatever you say,
I hold that song's worth all the bibelots
That people hail today with ah's and oh's.

ORONTE

And I maintain my sonnet's very good.

[Act One · Scene Two]

ALCESTE

It's not at all surprising that you should.
You have your reasons; permit me to have mine
For thinking that you cannot write a line.

ORONTE

Others have praised my sonnet to the skies.

ALCESTE

I lack their art of telling pleasant lies.

ORONTE

You seem to think you've got no end of wit.

ALCESTE

To praise your verse, I'd need still more of it.

ORONTE

I'm not in need of your approval, Sir.

ALCESTE

That's good; you couldn't have it if you were.

[Act One · Scene Two]

ORONTE

Come now, I'll lend you the subject of my sonnet;
I'd like to see you try to improve upon it.

ALCESTE

I might, by chance, write something just as shoddy;
But then I wouldn't show it to everybody.

ORONTE

You're most opinionated and conceited.

ALCESTE

Go find your flatterers, and be better treated.

ORONTE

Look here, my little fellow, pray watch your tone.

ALCESTE

My great big fellow, you'd better watch your own.

PHILINTE, *stepping between them*

Oh, please, please, gentlemen! This will never do.

[*Act One · Scene Two*]

ORONTE

The fault is mine, and I leave the field to you.
I am your servant, Sir, in every way.

ALCESTE

And I, Sir, am your most abject valet.

SCENE THREE

PHILINTE, ALCESTE

PHILINTE

Well, as you see, sincerity in excess
Can get you into a very pretty mess;
Oronte was hungry for appreciation. . . .

ALCESTE

Don't speak to me.

PHILINTE

What?

ALCESTE

No more conversation.

PHILINTE

Really, now . . .

[*Act One · Scene Three*]

ALCESTE

Leave me alone.

PHILINTE

If I . . .

ALCESTE

Out of my sight!

PHILINTE

But what . . .

ALCESTE

I won't listen.

PHILINTE

But . . .

ALCESTE

Silence!

PHILINTE

Now, is it polite . . .

[*Act One · Scene Three*]

ALCESTE

By heaven, I've had enough. Don't follow me.

PHILINTE

Ah, you're just joking. I'll keep you company.

Act 2

SCENE ONE

ALCESTE, CELIMENE

ALCESTE

Shall I speak plainly, Madam? I confess
Your conduct gives me infinite distress,
And my resentment's grown too hot to smother.
Soon, I foresee, we'll break with one another.
If I said otherwise, I should deceive you;
Sooner or later, I shall be forced to leave you,
And if I swore that we shall never part,
I should misread the omens of my heart.

CELIMENE

You kindly saw me home, it would appear,
So as to pour invectives in my ear.

ALCESTE

I've no desire to quarrel. But I deplore
Your inability to shut the door
On all these suitors who beset you so.
There's what annoys me, if you care to know.

[Act Two · Scene One]

CELIMENE

Is it my fault that all these men pursue me?
Am I to blame if they're attracted to me?
And when they gently beg an audience,
Ought I to take a stick and drive them hence?

ALCESTE

Madam, there's no necessity for a stick;
A less responsive heart would do the trick.
Of your attractiveness I don't complain;
But those your charms attract, you then detain
By a most melting and receptive manner,
And so enlist their hearts beneath your banner.
It's the agreeable hopes which you excite
That keep these lovers round you day and night;
Were they less liberally smiled upon,
That sighing troop would very soon be gone.
But tell me, Madam, why it is that lately
This man Clitandre interests you so greatly?
Because of what high merits do you deem
Him worthy of the honor of your esteem?
Is it that your admiring glances linger
On the splendidly long nail of his little finger?
Or do you share the general deep respect
For the blond wig he chooses to affect?
Are you in love with his embroidered hose?
Do you adore his ribbons and his bows?
Or is it that this paragon bewitches
Your tasteful eye with his vast German breeches?

[*Act Two · Scene One*]

Perhaps his giggle, or his falsetto voice,
Makes him the latest gallant of your choice?

CELIMENE

You're much mistaken to resent him so.
Why I put up with him you surely know:
My lawsuit's very shortly to be tried,
And I must have his influence on my side.

ALCESTE

Then lose your lawsuit, Madam, or let it drop;
Don't torture me by humoring such a fop.

CELIMENE

You're jealous of the whole world, Sir.

ALCESTE

                                      That's true,
Since the whole world is well-received by you.

CELIMENE

That my good nature is so unconfined
Should serve to pacify your jealous mind;
Were I to smile on one, and scorn the rest,
Then you might have some cause to be distressed.

[Act Two · Scene One]

ALCESTE

Well, if I mustn't be jealous, tell me, then,
Just how I'm better treated than other men.

CELIMENE

You know you have my love. Will that not do?

ALCESTE

What proof have I that what you say is true?

CELIMENE

I would expect, Sir, that my having said it
Might give the statement a sufficient credit.

ALCESTE

But how can I be sure that you don't tell
The selfsame thing to other men as well?

CELIMENE

What a gallant speech! How flattering to me!
What a sweet creature you make me out to be!
Well then, to save you from the pangs of doubt,
All that I've said I hereby cancel out;
Now, none but yourself shall make a monkey of you:
Are you content?

[Act Two · Scene One]

ALCESTE

              Why, why am I doomed to love you?
I swear that I shall bless the blissful hour
When this poor heart's no longer in your power!
I make no secret of it: I've done my best
To exorcise this passion from my breast;
But thus far all in vain; it will not go;
It's for my sins that I must love you so.

CELIMENE

Your love for me is matchless, Sir; that's clear.

ALCESTE

Indeed, in all the world it has no peer;
Words can't describe the nature of my passion,
And no man ever loved in such a fashion.

CELIMENE

Yes, it's a brand-new fashion, I agree:
You show your love by castigating me,
And all your speeches are enraged and rude.
I've never been so furiously wooed.

ALCESTE

Yet you could calm that fury, if you chose.
Come, shall we bring our quarrels to a close?
Let's speak with open hearts, then, and begin . . .

SCENE TWO

CELIMENE, ALCESTE, BASQUE

CELIMENE

What is it?

BASQUE

Acaste is here.

CELIMENE

Well, send him in.

SCENE THREE

CELIMENE, ALCESTE

ALCESTE

What! Shall we never be alone at all?
You're always ready to receive a call,
And you can't bear, for ten ticks of the clock,
Not to keep open house for all who knock.

CELIMENE

I couldn't refuse him: he'd be most put out.

ALCESTE

Surely that's not worth worrying about.

CELIMENE

Acaste would never forgive me if he guessed
That I consider him a dreadful pest.

ALCESTE

If he's a pest, why bother with him then?

[*Act Two · Scene Three*]

CELIMENE

Heavens! One can't antagonize such men;
Why, they're the chartered gossips of the court,
And have a say in things of every sort.
One must receive them, and be full of charm;
They're no great help, but they can do you harm,
And though your influence be ever so great,
They're hardly the best people to alienate.

ALCESTE

I see, dear lady, that you could make a case
For putting up with the whole human race;
These friendships that you calculate so nicely . . .

SCENE FOUR

ALCESTE, CELIMENE, BASQUE

BASQUE

Madam, Clitandre is here as well.

ALCESTE

Precisely.

CELIMENE

Where are you going?

ALCESTE

Elsewhere.

CELIMENE

Stay.

ALCESTE

No, no.

[*Act Two · Scene Four*]

CELIMENE

Stay, Sir.

ALCESTE

I can't.

CELIMENE

I wish it.

ALCESTE

No, I must go.
I beg you, Madam, not to press the matter;
You know I have no taste for idle chatter.

CELIMENE

Stay: I command you.

ALCESTE

No, I cannot stay.

CELIMENE

Very well; you have my leave to go away.

SCENE FIVE

ELIANTE, PHILINTE, ACASTE, CLITANDRE, ALCESTE, CELIMENE, BASQUE

ELIANTE, *to Célimène*

The Marquesses have kindly come to call.
Were they announced?

CELIMENE

Yes. Basque, bring chairs for all.
(*Basque provides the chairs, and exits.*)
(*To Alceste*)
You haven't gone?

ALCESTE

No; and I shan't depart
Till you decide who's foremost in your heart.

CELIMENE

Oh, hush.

ALCESTE

It's time to choose; take them, or me.

[Act Two · Scene Five]

CELIMENE

You're mad.

ALCESTE

I'm not, as you shall shortly see.

CELIMENE

Oh?

ALCESTE

You'll decide.

CELIMENE

You're joking now, dear friend.

ALCESTE

No, no; you'll choose; my patience is at an end.

CLITANDRE

Madam, I come from court, where poor Cléonte
Behaved like a perfect fool, as is his wont.
Has he no friend to counsel him, I wonder,
And teach him less unerringly to blunder?

CELIMENE

It's true, the man's a most accomplished dunce;
His gauche behavior charms the eye at once;

[*Act Two · Scene Five*]

And every time one sees him, on my word,
His manner's grown a trifle more absurd.

ACASTE

Speaking of dunces, I've just now conversed
With old Damon, who's one of the very worst;
I stood a lifetime in the broiling sun
Before his dreary monologue was done.

CELIMENE

Oh, he's a wondrous talker, and has the power
To tell you nothing hour after hour:
If, by mistake, he ever came to the point,
The shock would put his jawbone out of joint.

ELIANTE, *to Philinte*

The conversation takes its usual turn,
And all our dear friends' ears will shortly burn.

CLITANDRE

Timante's a character, Madam.

CELIMENE

                       Isn't he, though?
A man of mystery from top to toe,
Who moves about in a romantic mist
On secret missions which do not exist.

[*Act Two · Scene Five*]

His talk is full of eyebrows and grimaces;
How tired one gets of his momentous faces;
He's always whispering something confidential
Which turns out to be quite inconsequential;
Nothing's too slight for him to mystify;
He even whispers when he says "good-by."

ACASTE

Tell us about Géralde.

CELIMENE

                That tiresome ass.
He mixes only with the titled class,
And fawns on dukes and princes, and is bored
With anyone who's not at least a lord.
The man's obsessed with rank, and his discourses
Are all of hounds and carriages and horses;
He uses Christian names with all the great,
And the word Milord, with him, is out of date.

CLITANDRE

He's very taken with Bélise, I hear.

CELIMENE

She is the dreariest company, poor dear.
Whenever she comes to call, I grope about
To find some topic which will draw her out,
But, owing to her dry and faint replies,

[*Act Two · Scene Five*]

The conversation wilts, and droops, and dies.
In vain one hopes to animate her face
By mentioning the ultimate commonplace;
But sun or shower, even hail or frost
Are matters she can instantly exhaust.
Meanwhile her visit, painful though it is,
Drags on and on through mute eternities,
And though you ask the time, and yawn, and yawn,
She sits there like a stone and won't be gone.

ACASTE

Now for Adraste.

CELIMENE

          Oh, that conceited elf
Has a gigantic passion for himself;
He rails against the court, and cannot bear it
That none will recognize his hidden merit;
All honors given to others give offense
To his imaginary excellence.

CLITANDRE

What about young Cléon? His house, they say,
Is full of the best society, night and day.

CELIMENE

His cook has made him popular, not he:
It's Cléon's table that people come to see.

[*Act Two · Scene Five*]

ELIANTE

He gives a splendid dinner, you must admit.

CELIMENE

But must he serve himself along with it?
For my taste, he's a most insipid dish
Whose presence sours the wine and spoils the fish.

PHILINTE

Damis, his uncle, is admired no end.
What's your opinion, Madam?

CELIMENE

                    Why, he's my friend.

PHILINTE

He seems a decent fellow, and rather clever.

CELIMENE

He works too hard at cleverness, however.
I hate to see him sweat and struggle so
To fill his conversation with bons mots.
Since he's decided to become a wit
His taste's so pure that nothing pleases it;
He scolds at all the latest books and plays,

[*Act Two · Scene Five*]

Thinking that wit must never stoop to praise,
That finding fault's a sign of intellect,
That all appreciation is abject,
And that by damning everything in sight
One shows oneself in a distinguished light.
He's scornful even of our conversations:
Their trivial nature sorely tries his patience;
He folds his arms, and stands above the battle,
And listens sadly to our childish prattle.

ACASTE

Wonderful, Madam! You've hit him off precisely.

CLITANDRE

No one can sketch a character so nicely.

ALCESTE

How bravely, Sirs, you cut and thrust at all
These absent fools, till one by one they fall:
But let one come in sight, and you'll at once
Embrace the man you lately called a dunce,
Telling him in a tone sincere and fervent
How proud you are to be his humble servant.

CLITANDRE

Why pick on us? Madame's been speaking, Sir,
And you should quarrel, if you must, with her.

[*Act Two · Scene Five*]

ALCESTE

No, no, by God, the fault is yours, because
You lead her on with laughter and applause,
And make her think that she's the more delightful
The more her talk is scandalous and spiteful.
Oh, she would stoop to malice far, far less
If no such claque approved her cleverness.
It's flatterers like you whose foolish praise
Nourishes all the vices of these days.

PHILINTE

But why protest when someone ridicules
Those you'd condemn, yourself, as knaves or fools?

CELIMENE

Why, Sir? Because he loves to make a fuss.
You don't expect him to agree with us,
When there's an opportunity to express
His heaven-sent spirit of contrariness?
What other people think, he can't abide;
Whatever they say, he's on the other side;
He lives in deadly terror of agreeing;
'Twould make him seem an ordinary being.
Indeed, he's so in love with contradiction,
He'll turn against his most profound conviction
And with a furious eloquence deplore it,
If only someone else is speaking for it.

[Act Two · Scene Five]

ALCESTE

Go on, dear lady, mock me as you please;
You have your audience in ecstasies.

PHILINTE

But what she says is true: you have a way
Of bridling at whatever people say;
Whether they praise or blame, your angry spirit
Is equally unsatisfied to hear it.

ALCESTE

Men, Sir, are always wrong, and that's the reason
That righteous anger's never out of season;
All that I hear in all their conversation
Is flattering praise or reckless condemnation.

CELIMENE

But . . .

ALCESTE

No, no, Madam, I am forced to state
That you have pleasures which I deprecate,
And that these others, here, are much to blame
For nourishing the faults which are your shame.

CLITANDRE

I shan't defend myself, Sir; but I vow
I'd thought this lady faultless until now.

[*Act Two · Scene Five*]

ACASTE

I see her charms and graces, which are many;
But as for faults, I've never noticed any.

ALCESTE

I see them, Sir; and rather than ignore them,
I strenuously criticize her for them.
The more one loves, the more one should object
To every blemish, every least defect.
Were I this lady, I would soon get rid
Of lovers who approved of all I did,
And by their slack indulgence and applause
Endorsed my follies and excused my flaws.

CELIMENE

If all hearts beat according to your measure,
The dawn of love would be the end of pleasure;
And love would find its perfect consummation
In ecstasies of rage and reprobation.

ELIANTE

Love, as a rule, affects men otherwise,
And lovers rarely love to criticize.
They see their lady as a charming blur,
And find all things commendable in her.
If she has any blemish, fault, or shame,
They will redeem it by a pleasing name.
The pale-faced lady's lily-white, perforce;

[*Act Two · Scene Five*]

The swarthy one's a sweet brunette, of course;
The spindly lady has a slender grace;
The fat one has a most majestic pace;
The plain one, with her dress in disarray,
They classify as *beauté négligée;*
The hulking one's a goddess in their eyes,
The dwarf, a concentrate of Paradise;
The haughty lady has a noble mind;
The mean one's witty, and the dull one's kind;
The chatterbox has liveliness and verve,
The mute one has a virtuous reserve.
So lovers manage, in their passion's cause,
To love their ladies even for their flaws.

ALCESTE

But I still say . . .

CELIMENE

I think it would be nice
To stroll around the gallery once or twice.
What! You're not going, Sirs?

CLITANDRE AND ACASTE

No, Madam, no.

ALCESTE

You seem to be in terror lest they go.
Do what you will, Sirs; leave, or linger on,
But I shan't go till after you are gone.

[Act Two · Scene Five]

ACASTE

I'm free to linger, unless I should perceive
Madame is tired, and wishes me to leave.

CLITANDRE

And as for me, I needn't go today
Until the hour of the King's *coucher*.

CELIMENE, *to Alceste*

You're joking, surely?

ALCESTE

Not in the least; we'll see
Whether you'd rather part with them, or me.

SCENE SIX

ALCESTE, CELIMENE, ELIANTE, ACASTE, PHILINTE, CLITANDRE, BASQUE

BASQUE, *to Alceste*

Sir, there's a fellow here who bids me state
That he must see you, and that it can't wait.

ALCESTE

Tell him that I have no such pressing affairs.

BASQUE

It's a long tailcoat that this fellow wears,
With gold all over.

CELIMENE, *to Alceste*

You'd best go down and see.
Or—have him enter.

SCENE SEVEN

ALCESTE, CELIMENE, ELIANTE, ACASTE, PHILINTE, CLITANDRE, A GUARD of the Marshalsea

ALCESTE, *confronting the guard*

Well, what do you want with me? Come in, Sir.

GUARD

I've a word, Sir, for your ear.

ALCESTE

Speak it aloud, Sir; I shall strive to hear.

GUARD

The Marshals have instructed me to say
You must report to them without delay.

ALCESTE

Who? Me, Sir?

GUARD

Yes, Sir; you.

[Act Two · Scene Seven]

ALCESTE

> But what do they want?

PHILINTE, *to Alceste*

To scotch your silly quarrel with Oronte.

CELIMENE, *to Philinte*

What quarrel?

PHILINTE

> Oronte and he have fallen out
Over some verse he spoke his mind about;
The Marshals wish to arbitrate the matter.

ALCESTE

Never shall I equivocate or flatter!

PHILINTE

You'd best obey their summons; come, let's go.

ALCESTE

How can they mend our quarrel, I'd like to know?
Am I to make a cowardly retraction,
And praise those jingles to his satisfaction?
I'll not recant; I've judged that sonnet rightly.
It's bad.

[*Act Two · Scene Seven*]

PHILINTE

But you might say so more politely. . . .

ALCESTE

I'll not back down; his verses make me sick.

PHILINTE

If only you could be more politic!
But come, let's go.

ALCESTE

                I'll go, but I won't unsay
A single word.

PHILINTE

Well, let's be on our way.

ALCESTE

Till I am ordered by my lord the King
To praise that poem, I shall say the thing
Is scandalous, by God, and that the poet
Ought to be hanged for having the nerve to show it.
(*To Clitandre and Acaste, who are laughing*)
By heaven, Sirs, I really didn't know
That I was being humorous.

[Act Two · Scene Seven]

CELIMENE

                Go, Sir, go;
Settle your business.

ALCESTE

           I shall, and when I'm through,
I shall return to settle things with you.

Act 3

SCENE ONE

CLITANDRE, ACASTE

CLITANDRE

Dear Marquess, how contented you appear;
All things delight you, nothing mars your cheer.
Can you, in perfect honesty, declare
That you've a right to be so debonair?

ACASTE

By Jove, when I survey myself, I find
No cause whatever for distress of mind.
I'm young and rich; I can in modesty
Lay claim to an exalted pedigree;
And owing to my name and my condition
I shall not want for honors and position.
Then as to courage, that most precious trait,
I seem to have it, as was proved of late
Upon the field of honor, where my bearing,
They say, was very cool and rather daring.
I've wit, of course; and taste in such perfection
That I can judge without the least reflection,
And at the theater, which is my delight,
Can make or break a play on opening night,
And lead the crowd in hisses or bravos,

[*Act Three · Scene One*]

And generally be known as one who knows.
I'm clever, handsome, gracefully polite;
My waist is small, my teeth are strong and white;
As for my dress, the world's astonished eyes
Assure me that I bear away the prize.
I find myself in favor everywhere,
Honored by men, and worshiped by the fair;
And since these things are so, it seems to me
I'm justified in my complacency.

CLITANDRE

Well, if so many ladies hold you dear,
Why do you press a hopeless courtship here?

ACASTE

Hopeless, you say? I'm not the sort of fool
That likes his ladies difficult and cool.
Men who are awkward, shy, and peasantish
May pine for heartless beauties, if they wish,
Grovel before them, bear their cruelties,
Woo them with tears and sighs and bended knees,
And hope by dogged faithfulness to gain
What their poor merits never could obtain.
For men like me, however, it makes no sense
To love on trust, and foot the whole expense.
Whatever any lady's merits be,
I think, thank God, that I'm as choice as she;
That if my heart is kind enough to burn
For her, she owes me something in return;
And that in any proper love affair
The partners must invest an equal share.

[*Act Three · Scene One*]

CLITANDRE

You think, then, that our hostess favors you?

ACASTE

I've reason to believe that that is true.

CLITANDRE

How did you come to such a mad conclusion?
You're blind, dear fellow. This is sheer delusion.

ACASTE

All right, then: I'm deluded and I'm blind.

CLITANDRE

Whatever put the notion in your mind?

ACASTE

Delusion.

CLITANDRE

What persuades you that you're right?

ACASTE

I'm blind.

[*Act Three · Scene One*]

CLITANDRE

But have you any proofs to cite?

ACASTE

I tell you I'm deluded.

CLITANDRE

Have you, then,
Received some secret pledge from Célimène?

ACASTE

Oh, no: she scorns me.

CLITANDRE

Tell me the truth, I beg.

ACASTE

She just can't bear me.

CLITANDRE

Ah, don't pull my leg.
Tell me what hope she's given you, I pray.

[*Act Three · Scene One*]

ACASTE

I'm hopeless, and it's you who win the day.
She hates me thoroughly, and I'm so vexed
I mean to hang myself on Tuesday next.

CLITANDRE

Dear Marquess, let us have an armistice
And make a treaty. What do you say to this?
If ever one of us can plainly prove
That Célimène encourages his love,
The other must abandon hope, and yield,
And leave him in possession of the field.

ACASTE

Now, there's a bargain that appeals to me;
With all my heart, dear Marquess, I agree.
But hush.

SCENE TWO

CELIMENE, ACASTE, CLITANDRE

CELIMENE

Still here?

CLITANDRE

T'was love that stayed our feet.

CELIMENE

I think I heard a carriage in the street.
Whose is it? D'you know?

SCENE THREE

CELIMENE, ACASTE, CLITANDRE, BASQUE

BASQUE

Arsinoé is here, *Madame.*

CELIMENE

Arsinoé, you say? Oh, dear.

BASQUE

Eliante is entertaining her below.

CELIMENE

What brings the creature here, I'd like to know?

ACASTE

They say she's dreadfully prudish, but in fact
I think her piety . . .

[Act Three · Scene Three]

CELIMENE

     It's all an act.
At heart she's worldly, and her poor success
In snaring men explains her prudishness.
It breaks her heart to see the beaux and gallants
Engrossed by other women's charms and talents,
And so she's always in a jealous rage
Against the faulty standards of the age.
She lets the world believe that she's a prude
To justify her loveless solitude,
And strives to put a brand of moral shame
On all the graces that she cannot claim.
But still she'd love a lover; and Alceste
Appears to be the one she'd love the best.
His visits here are poison to her pride;
She seems to think I've lured him from her side;
And everywhere, at court or in the town,
The spiteful, envious woman runs me down.
In short, she's just as stupid as can be,
Vicious and arrogant in the last degree,
And . . .

SCENE FOUR

ARSINOE, CELIMENE, CLITANDRE, ACASTE

CELIMENE

Ah! What happy chance has brought you here?
I've thought about you ever so much, my dear.

ARSINOE

I've come to tell you something you should know.

CELIMENE

How good of you to think of doing so!
(*Clitandre and Acaste go out, laughing.*)

SCENE FIVE

ARSINOE, CELIMENE

ARSINOE

It's just as well those gentlemen didn't tarry.

CELIMENE

Shall we sit down?

ARSINOE

                That won't be necessary.
Madam, the flame of friendship ought to burn
Brightest in matters of the most concern,
And as there's nothing which concerns us more
Than honor, I have hastened to your door
To bring you, as your friend, some information
About the status of your reputation.
I visited, last night, some virtuous folk,
And, quite by chance, it was of you they spoke;
There was, I fear, no tendency to praise
Your light behavior and your dashing ways.
The quantity of gentlemen you see
And your by now notorious coquetry
Were both so vehemently criticized

[*Act Three · Scene Five*]

By everyone, that I was much surprised.
Of course, I needn't tell you where I stood;
I came to your defense as best I could,
Assured them you were harmless, and declared
Your soul was absolutely unimpaired.
But there are some things, you must realize,
One can't excuse, however hard one tries,
And I was forced at last into conceding
That your behavior, Madam, is misleading,
That it makes a bad impression, giving rise
To ugly gossip and obscene surmise,
And that if you were more *overtly* good,
You wouldn't be so much misunderstood.
Not that I think you've been unchaste—no! no!
The saints preserve me from a thought so low!
But mere good conscience never did suffice:
One must avoid the outward show of vice.
Madam, you're too intelligent, I'm sure,
To think my motives anything but pure
In offering you this counsel—which I do
Out of a zealous interest in you.

CELIMENE

Madam, I haven't taken you amiss;
I'm very much obliged to you for this;
And I'll at once discharge the obligation
By telling you about *your* reputation.
You've been so friendly as to let me know
What certain people say of me, and so
I mean to follow your benign example
By offering you a somewhat similar sample.

[Act Three · Scene Five]

The other day, I went to an affair
And found some most distinguished people there
Discussing piety, both false and true.
The conversation soon came round to you.
Alas! Your prudery and bustling zeal
Appeared to have a very slight appeal.
Your affectation of a grave demeanor,
Your endless talk of virtue and of honor,
The aptitude of your suspicious mind
For finding sin where there is none to find,
Your towering self-esteem, that pitying face
With which you contemplate the human race,
Your sermonizings and your sharp aspersions
On people's pure and innocent diversions—
All these were mentioned, Madam, and, in fact,
Were roundly and concertedly attacked.
"What good," they said, "are all these outward shows,
When everything belies her pious pose?
She prays incessantly; but then, they say,
She beats her maids and cheats them of their pay;
She shows her zeal in every holy place,
But still she's vain enough to paint her face;
She holds that naked statues are immoral,
But with a naked *man* she'd have no quarrel."
Of course, I said to everybody there
That they were being viciously unfair;
But still they were disposed to criticize you,
And all agreed that someone should advise you
To leave the morals of the world alone,
And worry rather more about your own.
They felt that one's self-knowledge should be great
Before one thinks of setting others straight;

[*Act Three · Scene Five*]

That one should learn the art of living well
Before one threatens other men with hell,
And that the Church is best equipped, no doubt,
To guide our souls and root our vices out.
Madam, you're too intelligent, I'm sure,
To think my motives anything but pure
In offering you this counsel—which I do
Out of a zealous interest in you.

ARSINOE

I dared not hope for gratitude, but I
Did not expect so acid a reply;
I judge, since you've been so extremely tart,
That my good counsel pierced you to the heart.

CELIMENE

Far from it, Madam. Indeed, it seems to me
We ought to trade advice more frequently.
One's vision of oneself is so defective
That it would be an excellent corrective.
If you are willing, Madam, let's arrange
Shortly to have another frank exchange
In which we'll tell each other, *entre nous*,
What you've heard tell of me, and I of you.

ARSINOE

Oh, people never censure you, my dear;
It's me they criticize. Or so I hear.

[*Act Three · Scene Five*]

CELIMENE

Madam, I think we either blame or praise
According to our taste and length of days.
There is a time of life for coquetry,
And there's a season, too, for prudery.
When all one's charms are gone, it is, I'm sure,
Good strategy to be devout and pure:
It makes one seem a little less forsaken.
Some day, perhaps, I'll take the road you've taken:
Time brings all things. But I have time aplenty,
And see no cause to be a prude at twenty.

ARSINOE

You give your age in such a gloating tone
That one would think I was an ancient crone;
We're not so far apart, in sober truth,
That you can mock me with a boast of youth!
Madam, you baffle me. I wish I knew
What moves you to provoke me as you do.

CELIMENE

For my part, Madam, I should like to know
Why you abuse me everywhere you go.
Is it my fault, dear lady, that your hand
Is not, alas, in very great demand?
If men admire me, if they pay me court
And daily make me offers of the sort

[*Act Three · Scene Five*]

You'd dearly love to have them make to you,
How can I help it? What would you have me do?
If what you want is lovers, please feel free
To take as many as you can from me.

ARSINOE

Oh, come. D'you think the world is losing sleep
Over that flock of lovers which you keep,
Or that we find it difficult to guess
What price you pay for their devotedness?
Surely you don't expect us to suppose
Mere merit could attract so many beaux?
It's not your virtue that they're dazzled by;
Nor is it virtuous love for which they sigh.
You're fooling no one, Madam; the world's not blind;
There's many a lady heaven has designed
To call men's noblest, tenderest feelings out,
Who has no lovers dogging her about;
From which it's plain that lovers nowadays
Must be acquired in bold and shameless ways,
And only pay one court for such reward
As modesty and virtue can't afford.
Then don't be quite so puffed up, if you please,
About your tawdry little victories;
Try, if you can, to be a shade less vain,
And treat the world with somewhat less disdain.
If one were envious of your amours,
One soon could have a following like yours;
Lovers are no great trouble to collect
If one prefers them to one's self-respect.

[*Act Three · Scene Five*]

CELIMENE

Collect them then, my dear; I'd love to see
You demonstrate that charming theory;
Who knows, you might . . .

ARSINOE

                Now, Madam, that will do;
It's time to end this trying interview.
My coach is late in coming to your door,
Or I'd have taken leave of you before.

CELIMENE

Oh, please don't feel that you must rush away;
I'd be delighted, Madam, if you'd stay.
However, lest my conversation bore you,
Let me provide some better company for you;
This gentleman, who comes most apropos,
Will please you more than I could do, I know.

SCENE SIX

ALCESTE, CELIMENE, ARSINOE

CELIMENE

Alceste, I have a little note to write
Which simply must go out before tonight;
Please entertain *Madame*; I'm sure that she
Will overlook my incivility.

SCENE SEVEN

ALCESTE, ARSINOE

ARSINOE

Well, Sir, our hostess graciously contrives
For us to chat until my coach arrives;
And I shall be forever in her debt
For granting me this little tête-à-tête.
We women very rightly give our hearts
To men of noble character and parts,
And your especial merits, dear Alceste,
Have roused the deepest sympathy in my breast.
Oh, how I wish they had sufficient sense
At court, to recognize your excellence!
They wrong you greatly, Sir. How it must hurt you
Never to be rewarded for your virtue!

ALCESTE

Why, Madam, what cause have I to feel aggrieved?
What great and brilliant thing have I achieved?
What service have I rendered to the King
That I should look to him for anything?

[*Act Three · Scene Seven*]

ARSINOE

Not everyone who's honored by the State
Has done great services. A man must wait
Till time and fortune offer him the chance.
Your merit, Sir, is obvious at a glance,
And . . .

ALCESTE

Ah, forget my merit; I'm not neglected.
The court, I think, can hardly be expected
To mine men's souls for merit, and unearth
Our hidden virtues and our secret worth.

ARSINOE

Some virtues, though, are far too bright to hide;
Yours are acknowledged, Sir, on every side.
Indeed, I've heard you warmly praised of late
By persons of considerable weight.

ALCESTE

This fawning age has praise for everyone,
And all distinctions, Madam, are undone.
All things have equal honor nowadays,
And no one should be gratified by praise.
To be admired, one only need exist,
And every lackey's on the honors list.

[Act Three · Scene Seven]

ARSINOE

I only wish, Sir, that you had your eye
On some position at court, however high;
You'd only have to hint at such a notion
For me to set the proper wheels in motion;
I've certain friendships I'd be glad to use
To get you any office you might choose.

ALCESTE

Madam, I fear that any such ambition
Is wholly foreign to my disposition.
The soul God gave me isn't of the sort
That prospers in the weather of a court.
It's all too obvious that I don't possess
The virtues necessary for success.
My one great talent is for speaking plain;
I've never learned to flatter or to feign;
And anyone so stupidly sincere
Had best not seek a courtier's career.
Outside the court, I know, one must dispense
With honors, privilege, and influence;
But still one gains the right, foregoing these,
Not to be tortured by the wish to please.
One needn't live in dread of snubs and slights,
Nor praise the verse that every idiot writes,
Nor humor silly Marquesses, nor bestow
Politic sighs on Madam So-and-So.

ARSINOE

Forget the court, then; let the matter rest.
But I've another cause to be distressed

[*Act Three · Scene Seven*]

About your present situation, Sir.
It's to your love affair that I refer.
She whom you love, and who pretends to love you,
Is, I regret to say, unworthy of you.

ALCESTE

Why, Madam! Can you seriously intend
To make so grave a charge against your friend?

ARSINOE

Alas, I must. I've stood aside too long
And let that lady do you grievous wrong;
But now my debt to conscience shall be paid:
I tell you that your love has been betrayed.

ALCESTE

I thank you, Madam; you're extremely kind.
Such words are soothing to a lover's mind.

ARSINOE

Yes, though she *is* my friend, I say again
You're very much too good for Célimène.
She's wantonly misled you from the start.

ALCESTE

You may be right; who knows another's heart?
But ask yourself if it's the part of charity
To shake my soul with doubts of her sincerity.

[*Act Three · Scene Seven*]

ARSINOE

Well, if you'd rather be a dupe than doubt her,
That's your affair. I'll say no more about her.

ALCESTE

Madam, you know that doubt and vague suspicion
Are painful to a man in my position;
It's most unkind to worry me this way
Unless you've some real proof of what you say.

ARSINOE

Sir, say no more: all doubt shall be removed,
And all that I've been saying shall be proved.
You've only to escort me home, and there
We'll look into the heart of this affair.
I've ocular evidence which will persuade you
Beyond a doubt, that Célimène's betrayed you.
Then, if you're saddened by that revelation,
Perhaps I can provide some consolation.

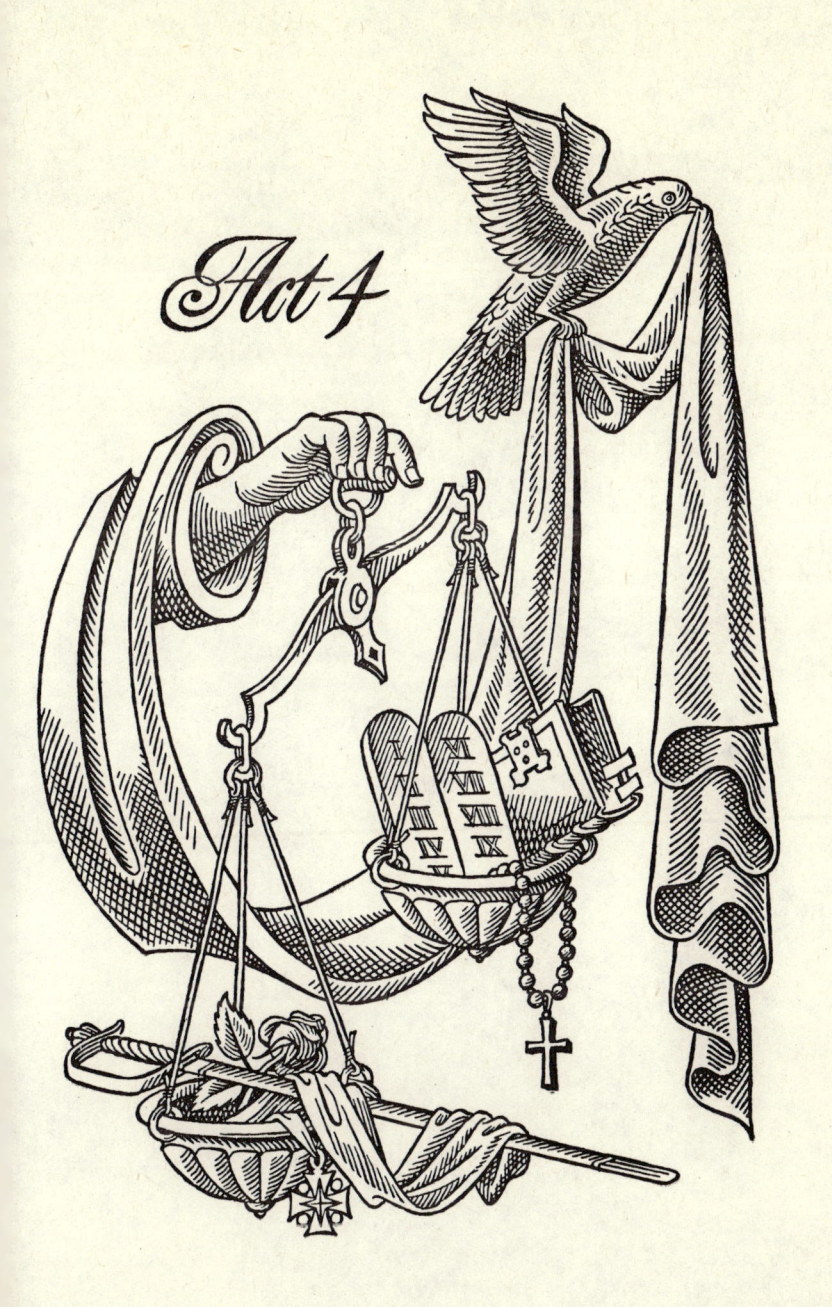

Act 4

SCENE ONE

ELIANTE, PHILINTE

PHILINTE

Madam, he acted like a stubborn child;
I thought they never would be reconciled;
In vain we reasoned, threatened, and appealed;
He stood his ground and simply would not yield.
The Marshals, I feel sure, have never heard
An argument so splendidly absurd.
"No, gentlemen," said he, "I'll not retract.
His verse is bad: extremely bad, in fact.
Surely it does the man no harm to know it.
Does it disgrace him, not to be a poet?
A gentleman may be respected still,
Whether he writes a sonnet well or ill.
That I dislike his verse should not offend him;
In all that touches honor, I commend him;
He's noble, brave, and virtuous—but I fear
He can't in truth be called a sonneteer.
I'll gladly praise his wardrobe; I'll endorse
His dancing, or the way he sits a horse;
But, gentlemen, I cannot praise his rhyme.
In fact, it ought to be a capital crime
For anyone so sadly unendowed
To write a sonnet, and read the thing aloud."

[Act Four · Scene One]

At length he fell into a gentler mood
And, striking a concessive attitude,
He paid Oronte the following courtesies:
"Sir, I regret that I'm so hard to please,
And I'm profoundly sorry that your lyric
Failed to provoke me to a panegyric."
After these curious words, the two embraced,
And then the hearing was adjourned—in haste.

ELIANTE

His conduct has been very singular lately;
Still, I confess that I respect him greatly.
The honesty in which he takes such pride
Has—to my mind—its noble, heroic side.
In this false age, such candor seems outrageous;
But I could wish that it were more contagious.

PHILINTE

What most intrigues me in our friend Alceste
Is the grand passion that rages in his breast.
The sullen humors he's compounded of
Should not, I think, dispose his heart to love;
But since they do, it puzzles me still more
That he should choose your cousin to adore.

ELIANTE

It does, indeed, belie the theory
That love is born of gentle sympathy,
And that the tender passion must be based
On sweet accords of temper and of taste.

[Act Four · Scene One]

PHILINTE

Does she return his love, do you suppose?

ELIANTE

Ah, that's a difficult question, Sir. Who knows?
How can we judge the truth of her devotion?
Her heart's a stranger to its own emotion.
Sometimes it thinks it loves, when no love's there;
At other times it loves quite unaware.

PHILINTE

I rather think Alceste is in for more
Distress and sorrow than he's bargained for;
Were he of my mind, Madam, his affection
Would turn in quite a different direction,
And we would see him more responsive to
The kind regard which he receives from you.

ELIANTE

Sir, I believe in frankness, and I'm inclined,
In matters of the heart, to speak my mind.
I don't oppose his love for her; indeed,
I hope with all my heart that he'll succeed,
And were it in my power, I'd rejoice
In giving him the lady of his choice.
But if, as happens frequently enough
In love affairs, he meets with a rebuff—
If Célimène should grant some rival's suit—

[*Act Four · Scene One*]

I'd gladly play the role of substitute;
Nor would his tender speeches please me less
Because they'd once been made without success.

PHILINTE

Well, Madam, as for me, I don't oppose
Your hopes in this affair; and heaven knows
That in my conversations with the man
I plead your cause as often as I can.
But if those two should marry, and so remove
All chance that he will offer you his love,
Then I'll declare my own, and hope to see
Your gracious favor pass from him to me.
In short, should you be cheated of Alceste,
I'd be most happy to be second best.

ELIANTE

Philinte, you're teasing.

PHILINTE

              Ah, Madam, never fear;
No words of mine were ever so sincere,
And I shall live in fretful expectation
Till I can make a fuller declaration.

SCENE TWO

ALCESTE, ELIANTE, PHILINTE

ALCESTE

Avenge me, Madam! I must have satisfaction,
Or this great wrong will drive me to distraction!

ELIANTE

Why, what's the matter? What's upset you so?

ALCESTE

Madam, I've had a mortal, mortal blow.
If Chaos repossessed the universe,
I swear I'd not be shaken any worse.
I'm ruined. . . . I can say no more. . . . My soul . . .

ELIANTE

Do try, Sir, to regain your self-control.

ALCESTE

Just heaven! Why were so much beauty and grace
Bestowed on one so vicious and so base?

[*Act Four · Scene Two*]

ELIANTE

Once more, Sir, tell us. . . .

ALCESTE

                   My world has gone to wrack;
I'm—I'm betrayed; she's stabbed me in the back:
Yes, Célimène (who would have thought it of her?)
Is false to me, and has another lover.

ELIANTE

Are you quite certain? Can you prove these things?

PHILINTE

Lovers are prey to wild imaginings
And jealous fancies. No doubt there's some mistake. . . .

ALCESTE

Mind your own business, Sir, for heaven's sake.
(*To Eliante*)
Madam, I have the proof that you demand
Here in my pocket, penned by her own hand.
Yes, all the shameful evidence one could want
Lies in this letter written to Oronte—
Oronte! whom I felt sure she couldn't love,
And hardly bothered to be jealous of.

[Act Four · Scene Two]

PHILINTE

Still, in a letter, appearances may deceive;
This may not be so bad as you believe.

ALCESTE

Once more I beg you, Sir, to let me be;
Tend to your own affairs; leave mine to me.

ELIANTE

Compose yourself; this anguish that you feel . . .

ALCESTE

Is something, Madam, you alone can heal.
My outraged heart, beside itself with grief,
Appeals to you for comfort and relief.
Avenge me on your cousin, whose unjust
And faithless nature has deceived my trust;
Avenge a crime your pure soul must detest.

ELIANTE

But how, Sir?

ALCESTE

      Madam, this heart within my breast
Is yours; pray take it; redeem my heart from her,
And so avenge me on my torturer.

[Act Four · Scene Two]

Let her be punished by the fond emotion,
The ardent love, the bottomless devotion,
The faithful worship which this heart of mine
Will offer up to yours as to a shrine.

ELIANTE

You have my sympathy, Sir, in all you suffer;
Nor do I scorn the noble heart you offer;
But I suspect you'll soon be mollified,
And this desire for vengeance will subside.
When some beloved hand has done us wrong
We thirst for retribution—but not for long;
However dark the deed that she's committed,
A lovely culprit's very soon acquitted.
Nothing's so stormy as an injured lover,
And yet no storm so quickly passes over.

ALCESTE

No, Madam, no—this is no lovers' spat;
I'll not forgive her; it's gone too far for that;
My mind's made up; I'll kill myself before
I waste my hopes upon her any more.
Ah, here she is. My wrath intensifies.
I shall confront her with her tricks and lies,
And crush her utterly, and bring you then
A heart no longer slave to Célimène.

SCENE THREE

CELIMENE, ALCESTE

ALCESTE, *aside*

Sweet heaven, help me to control my passion.

CELIMENE

(*Aside*)
    (*To Alceste*)
Oh, Lord. Why stand there staring in that fashion?
And what d'you mean by those dramatic sighs,
And that malignant glitter in your eyes?

ALCESTE

I mean that sins which cause the blood to freeze
Look innocent beside your treacheries;
That nothing Hell's or Heaven's wrath could do
Ever produced so bad a thing as you.

CELIMENE

Your compliments were always sweet and pretty.

[*Act Four · Scene Three*]

ALCESTE

Madam, it's not the moment to be witty.
No, blush and hang your head; you've ample reason,
Since I've the fullest evidence of your treason.
Ah, this is what my sad heart prophesied;
Now all my anxious fears are verified;
My dark suspicion and my gloomy doubt
Divined the truth, and now the truth is out.
For all your trickery, I was not deceived;
It was my bitter stars that I believed.
But don't imagine that you'll go scot-free;
You shan't misuse me with impunity.
I know that love's irrational and blind;
I know the heart's not subject to the mind,
And can't be reasoned into beating faster;
I know each soul is free to choose its master;
Therefore had you but spoken from the heart,
Rejecting my attentions from the start,
I'd have no grievance, or at any rate
I could complain of nothing but my fate.
Ah, but so falsely to encourage me—
That was a treason and a treachery
For which you cannot suffer too severely,
And you shall pay for that behavior dearly.
Yes, now I have no pity, not a shred;
My temper's out of hand; I've lost my head;
Shocked by the knowledge of your double-dealings,
My reason can't restrain my savage feelings;
A righteous wrath deprives me of my senses,
And I won't answer for the consequences.

[Act Four · Scene Three]

CELIMENE

What does this outburst mean? Will you please explain?
Have you, by any chance, gone quite insane?

ALCESTE

Yes, yes, I went insane the day I fell
A victim to your black and fatal spell,
Thinking to meet with some sincerity
Among the treacherous charms that beckoned me.

CELIMENE

Pooh. Of what treachery can you complain?

ALCESTE

How sly you are, how cleverly you feign!
But you'll not victimize me any more.
Look: here's a document you've seen before.
This evidence, which I acquired today,
Leaves you, I think, without a thing to say.

CELIMENE

Is this what sent you into such a fit?

ALCESTE

You should be blushing at the sight of it.

[*Act Four · Scene Three*]

CELIMENE

Ought I to blush? I truly don't see why.

ALCESTE

Ah, now you're being bold as well as sly;
Since there's no signature, perhaps you'll claim . . .

CELIMENE

I wrote it, whether or not it bears my name.

ALCESTE

And you can view with equanimity
This proof of your disloyalty to me!

CELIMENE

Oh, don't be so outrageous and extreme.

ALCESTE

You take this matter lightly, it would seem.
Was it no wrong to me, no shame to you,
That you should send Oronte this billet-doux?

CELIMENE

Oronte! Who said it was for him?

[Act Four · Scene Three]

ALCESTE

> Why, those
Who brought me this example of your prose.
But what's the difference? If you wrote the letter
To someone else, it pleases me no better.
My grievance and your guilt remain the same.

CELIMENE

But need you rage, and need I blush for shame,
If this was written to a *woman* friend?

ALCESTE

Ah! Most ingenious. I'm impressed no end;
And after that incredible evasion
Your guilt is clear. I need no more persuasion.
How dare you try so clumsy a deception?
D'you think I'm wholly wanting in perception?
Come, come, let's see how brazenly you'll try
To bolster up so palpable a lie:
Kindly construe this ardent closing section
As nothing more than sisterly affection!
Here, let me read it. Tell me, if you dare to,
That this is for a woman . . .

CELIMENE

> I don't care to.
What right have you to badger and berate me,
And so highhandedly interrogate me?

[*Act Four · Scene Three*]

ALCESTE

Now, don't be angry; all I ask of you
Is that you justify a phrase or two . . .

CELIMENE

No, I shall not. I utterly refuse,
And you may take those phrases as you choose.

ALCESTE

Just show me how this letter could be meant
For a woman's eyes, and I shall be content.

CELIMENE

No, no, it's for Oronte; you're perfectly right.
I welcome his attentions with delight,
I prize his character and his intellect,
And everything is just as you suspect.
Come, do your worst now; give your rage free rein;
But kindly cease to bicker and complain.

ALCESTE, *aside*

Good God! Could anything be more inhuman?
Was ever a heart so mangled by a woman?
When I complain of how she has betrayed me,
She bridles, and commences to upbraid me!
She tries my tortured patience to the limit;
She won't deny her guilt; she glories in it!

[Act Four · Scene Three]

And yet my heart's too faint and cowardly
To break these chains of passion, and be free,
To scorn her as it should, and rise above
This unrewarded, mad, and bitter love.
(*To Célimène*)
Ah, traitress, in how confident a fashion
You take advantage of my helpless passion,
And use my weakness for your faithless charms
To make me once again throw down my arms!
But do at least deny this black transgression;
Take back that mocking and perverse confession;
Defend this letter and your innocence,
And I, poor fool, will aid in your defense.
Pretend, pretend, that you are just and true,
And I shall make myself believe in you.

CELIMENE

Oh, stop it. Don't be such a jealous dunce,
Or I shall leave off loving you at once.
Just why should I *pretend*? What could impel me
To stoop so low as that? And kindly tell me
Why, if I loved another, I shouldn't merely
Inform you of it, simply and sincerely!
I've told you where you stand, and that admission
Should altogether clear me of suspicion;
After so generous a guarantee,
What right have you to harbor doubts of me?
Since women are (from natural reticence)
Reluctant to declare their sentiments,
And since the honor of our sex requires
That we conceal our amorous desires,

[*Act Four · Scene Three*]

Ought any man for whom such laws are broken
To question what the oracle has spoken?
Should he not rather feel an obligation
To trust that most obliging declaration?
Enough, now. Your suspicions quite disgust me;
Why should I love a man who doesn't trust me?
I cannot understand why I continue,
Fool that I am, to take an interest in you.
I ought to choose a man less prone to doubt,
And give you something to be vexed about.

ALCESTE

Ah, what a poor enchanted fool I am;
These gentle words, no doubt, were all a sham;
But destiny requires me to entrust
My happiness to you, and so I must.
I'll love you to the bitter end, and see
How false and treacherous you dare to be.

CELIMENE

No, you don't really love me as you ought.

ALCESTE

I love you more than can be said or thought;
Indeed, I wish you were in such distress
That I might show my deep devotedness.
Yes, I could wish that you were wretchedly poor,
Unloved, uncherished, utterly obscure;
That fate had set you down upon the earth

[*Act Four · Scene Three*]

Without possessions, rank, or gentle birth;
Then, by the offer of my heart, I might
Repair the great injustice of your plight;
I'd raise you from the dust, and proudly prove
The purity and vastness of my love.

CELIMENE

This is a strange benevolence indeed!
God grant that I may never be in need. . . .
Ah, here's Monsieur Dubois, in quaint disguise.

SCENE FOUR

CELIMENE, ALCESTE, DUBOIS

ALCESTE

Well, why this costume? Why those frightened eyes?
What ails you?

DUBOIS

Well, Sir, things are most mysterious.

ALCESTE

What do you mean?

DUBOIS

I fear they're very serious.

ALCESTE

What?

DUBOIS

Shall I speak more loudly?

[*Act Four · Scene Four*]

ALCESTE

Yes; speak out.

DUBOIS

Isn't there someone here, Sir?

ALCESTE

Speak, you lout!
Stop wasting time.

DUBOIS

Sir, we must slip away.

ALCESTE

How's that?

DUBOIS

We must decamp without delay.

ALCESTE

Explain yourself.

DUBOIS

I tell you we must fly.

[*Act Four · Scene Four*]

ALCESTE

What for?

DUBOIS

We mustn't pause to say good-by.

ALCESTE

Now what d'you mean by all of this, you clown?

DUBOIS

I mean, Sir, that we've got to leave this town.

ALCESTE

I'll tear you limb from limb and joint from joint
If you don't come more quickly to the point.

DUBOIS

Well, Sir, today a man in a black suit,
Who wore a black and ugly scowl to boot,
Left us a document scrawled in such a hand
As even Satan couldn't understand.

[Act Four · Scene Four]

It bears upon your lawsuit, I don't doubt;
But all hell's devils couldn't make it out.

ALCESTE

Well, well, go on. What then? I fail to see
How this event obliges us to flee.

DUBOIS

Well, Sir: an hour later, hardly more,
A gentleman who's often called before
Came looking for you in an anxious way.
Not finding you, he asked me to convey
(Knowing I could be trusted with the same)
The following message. . . . Now, what *was* his name?

ALCESTE

Forget his name, you idiot. What did he say?

DUBOIS

Well, it was one of your friends, Sir, anyway.
He warned you to begone, and he suggested
That if you stay, you may well be arrested.

ALCESTE

What? Nothing more specific? Think, man, think!

[*Act Four · Scene Four*]

DUBOIS

No, Sir. He had me bring him pen and ink,
And dashed you off a letter which, I'm sure,
Will render things distinctly less obscure.

ALCESTE

Well—let me have it!

CELIMENE

What *is* this all about?

ALCESTE

God knows; but I have hopes of finding out.
How long am I to wait, you blitherer?

DUBOIS, *after a protracted search for the letter*

I must have left it on your table, Sir.

ALCESTE

I ought to . . .

CELIMENE

No, no, keep your self-control;
Go find out what's behind his rigmarole.

[*Act Four · Scene Four*]

ALCESTE

It seems that fate, no matter what I do,
Has sworn that I may not converse with you;
But, Madam, pray permit your faithful lover
To try once more before the day is over.

Act 5

SCENE ONE

ALCESTE, PHILINTE

ALCESTE

No, it's too much. My mind's made up, I tell you.

PHILINTE

Why should this blow, however hard, compel you . . .

ALCESTE

No, no, don't waste your breath in argument;
Nothing you say will alter my intent;
This age is vile, and I've made up my mind
To have no further commerce with mankind.
Did not truth, honor, decency, and the laws
Oppose my enemy and approve my cause?
My claims were justified in all men's sight;
I put my trust in equity and right;
Yet, to my horror and the world's disgrace,
Justice is mocked, and I have lost my case!
A scoundrel whose dishonesty is notorious
Emerges from another lie victorious!
Honor and right condone his brazen fraud,
While rectitude and decency applaud!

[Act Five · Scene One]

Before his smirking face, the truth stands charmed,
And virtue conquered, and the law disarmed!
His crime is sanctioned by a court decree!
And not content with what he's done to me,
The dog now seeks to ruin me by stating
That I composed a book now circulating,
A book so wholly criminal and vicious
That even to speak its title is seditious!
Meanwhile Oronte, my rival, lends his credit
To the same libelous tale, and helps to spread it!
Oronte! a man of honor and of rank,
With whom I've been entirely fair and frank;
Who sought me out and forced me, willy-nilly,
To judge some verse I found extremely silly;
And who, because I properly refused
To flatter him, or see the truth abused,
Abets my enemy in a rotten slander!
There's the reward of honesty and candor!
The man will hate me to the end of time
For failing to commend his wretched rhyme!
And not this man alone, but all humanity
Do what they do from interest and vanity;
They prate of honor, truth, and righteousness,
But lie, betray, and swindle nonetheless.
Come then: man's villainy is too much to bear;
Let's leave this jungle and this jackal's lair.
Yes! treacherous and savage race of men,
You shall not look upon my face again.

PHILINTE

Oh, don't rush into exile prematurely;
Things aren't as dreadful as you make them, surely.

[Act Five · Scene One]

It's rather obvious, since you're still at large,
That people don't believe your enemy's charge.
Indeed, his tale's so patently untrue
That it may do more harm to him than you.

ALCESTE

Nothing could do that scoundrel any harm:
His frank corruption is his greatest charm,
And, far from hurting him, a further shame
Would only serve to magnify his name.

PHILINTE

In any case, his bald prevarication
Has done no injury to your reputation,
And you may feel secure in that regard.
As for your lawsuit, it should not be hard
To have the case reopened, and contest
This judgment . . .

ALCESTE

                  No, no, let the verdict rest.
Whatever cruel penalty it may bring,
I wouldn't have it changed for anything.
It shows the times' injustice with such clarity
That I shall pass it down to our posterity
As a great proof and signal demonstration
Of the black wickedness of this generation.
It may cost twenty thousand francs; but I

[Act Five · Scene One]

Shall pay their twenty thousand, and gain thereby
The right to storm and rage at human evil,
And send the race of mankind to the devil.

PHILINTE

Listen to me. . . .

ALCESTE

Why? What can you possibly say?
Don't argue, Sir; your labor's thrown away.
Do you propose to offer lame excuses
For men's behavior and the times' abuses?

PHILINTE

No, all you say I'll readily concede:
This is a low, dishonest age indeed;
Nothing but trickery prospers nowadays,
And people ought to mend their shabby ways.
Yes, man's a beastly creature; but must we then
Abandon the society of men?
Here in the world, each human frailty
Provides occasion for philosophy,
And that is virtue's noblest exercise;
If honesty shone forth from all men's eyes,
If every heart were frank and kind and just,
What could our virtues do but gather dust
(Since their employment is to help us bear
The villainies of men without despair)?
A heart well-armed with virtue can endure. . . .

[*Act Five · Scene One*]

ALCESTE

Sir, you're a matchless reasoner, to be sure;
Your words are fine and full of cogency;
But don't waste time and eloquence on me.
My reason bids me go, for my own good.
My tongue won't lie and flatter as it should;
God knows what frankness it might next commit,
And what I'd suffer on account of it.
Pray let me wait for Célimène's return
In peace and quiet. I shall shortly learn,
By her response to what I have in view,
Whether her love for me is feigned or true.

PHILINTE

Till then, let's visit Eliante upstairs.

ALCESTE

No, I am too weighed down with somber cares.
Go to her, do; and leave me with my gloom
Here in the darkened corner of this room.

PHILINTE

Why, that's no sort of company, my friend;
I'll see if Eliante will not descend.

SCENE TWO

CELIMENE, ORONTE, ALCESTE

ORONTE

Yes, Madam, if you wish me to remain
Your true and ardent lover, you must deign
To give me some more positive assurance.
All this suspense is quite beyond endurance.
If your heart shares the sweet desires of mine,
Show me as much by some convincing sign;
And here's the sign I urgently suggest:
That you no longer tolerate Alceste,
But sacrifice him to my love, and sever
All your relations with the man forever.

CELIMENE

Why do you suddenly dislike him so?
You praised him to the skies not long ago.

ORONTE

Madam, that's not the point. I'm here to find
Which way your tender feelings are inclined.
Choose, if you please, between Alceste and me,
And I shall stay or go accordingly.

[Act Five · Scene Two]

ALCESTE, *emerging from the corner*

Yes, Madam, choose; this gentleman's demand
Is wholly just, and I support his stand.
I too am true and ardent; I too am here
To ask you that you make your feelings clear.
No more delays, now; no equivocation;
The time has come to make your declaration.

ORONTE

Sir, I've no wish in any way to be
An obstacle to your felicity.

ALCESTE

Sir, I've no wish to share her heart with you;
That may sound jealous, but at least it's true.

ORONTE

If, weighing us, she leans in your direction . . .

ALCESTE

If she regards you with the least affection . . .

ORONTE

I swear I'll yield her to you there and then.

[Act Five · Scene Two]

ALCESTE

I swear I'll never see her face again.

ORONTE

Now, Madam, tell us what we've come to hear.

ALCESTE

Madam, speak openly and have no fear.

ORONTE

Just say which one is to remain your lover.

ALCESTE

Just name one name, and it will all be over.

ORONTE

What! Is it possible that you're undecided?

ALCESTE

What! Can your feelings possibly be divided?

CELIMENE

Enough: this inquisition's gone too far:
How utterly unreasonable you are!
Not that I couldn't make the choice with ease;

[*Act Five · Scene Two*]

My heart has no conflicting sympathies;
I know full well which one of you I favor,
And you'd not see me hesitate or waver.
But how can you expect me to reveal
So cruelly and bluntly what I feel?
I think it altogether too unpleasant
To choose between two men when both are present;
One's heart has means more subtle and more kind
Of letting its affections be divined,
Nor need one be uncharitably plain
To let a lover know he loves in vain.

ORONTE

No, no, speak plainly; I for one can stand it.
I beg you to be frank.

ALCESTE

              And I demand it.
The simple truth is what I wish to know,
And there's no need for softening the blow.
You've made an art of pleasing everyone,
But now your days of coquetry are done:
You have no choice now, Madam, but to choose,
For I'll know what to think if you refuse;
I'll take your silence for a clear admission
That I'm entitled to my worst suspicion.

ORONTE

I thank you for this ultimatum, Sir,
And I may say I heartily concur.

[*Act Five · Scene Two*]

CELIMENE

Really, this foolishness is very wearing:
Must you be so unjust and overbearing?
Haven't I told you why I must demur?
Ah, here's Eliante; I'll put the case to her.

SCENE THREE

ELIANTE, PHILINTE, CELIMENE, ORONTE, ALCESTE

CELIMENE

Cousin, I'm being persecuted here
By these two persons, who, it would appear,
Will not be satisfied till I confess
Which one I love the more, and which the less,
And tell the latter to his face that he
Is henceforth banished from my company.
Tell me, has ever such a thing been done?

ELIANTE

You'd best not turn to me; I'm not the one
To back you in a matter of this kind:
I'm all for those who frankly speak their mind.

ORONTE

Madam, you'll search in vain for a defender.

ALCESTE

You're beaten, Madam, and may as well surrender.

[Act Five · Scene Three]

ORONTE

Speak, speak, you must; and end this awful strain.

ALCESTE

Or don't, and your position will be plain.

ORONTE

A single word will close this painful scene.

ALCESTE

But if you're silent, I'll know what you mean.

SCENE FOUR

**ARSINOE, CELIMENE, ELIANTE,
ALCESTE, PHILINTE,
ACASTE, CLITANDRE, ORONTE**

ACASTE, *to Célimène*

Madam, with all due deference, we two
Have come to pick a little bone with you.

CLITANDRE, *to Oronte and Alceste*

I'm glad you're present, Sirs; as you'll soon learn,
Our business here is also your concern.

ARSINOE, *to Célimène*

Madam, I visit you so soon again
Only because of these two gentlemen,
Who came to me indignant and aggrieved
About a crime too base to be believed.
Knowing your virtue, having such confidence in it,
I couldn't think you guilty for a minute,
In spite of all their telling evidence;
And, rising above our little difference,
I've hastened here in friendship's name to see
You clear yourself of this great calumny.

[Act Five · Scene Four]

ACASTE

Yes, Madam, let us see with what composure
You'll manage to respond to this disclosure.
You lately sent Clitandre this tender note.

CLITANDRE

And this one, for Acaste, you also wrote.

ACASTE, *to Oronte and Alceste*

You'll recognize this writing, Sirs, I think;
The lady is so free with pen and ink
That you must know it all too well, I fear.
But listen: this is something you should hear.

"How absurd you are to condemn my lightheartedness in society, and to accuse me of being happiest in the company of others. Nothing could be more unjust; and if you do not come to me instantly and beg pardon for saying such a thing, I shall never forgive you as long as I live. Our big bumbling friend the Viscount . . ."

What a shame that he's not here.

"Our big bumbling friend the Viscount, whose name stands first in your complaint, is hardly a man to my taste; and ever since the day I watched him spend three-quarters of an hour spitting into a well, so as to make circles in the water, I have been unable to think highly of him. As for the little Marquess . . ."

In all modesty, gentlemen, that is I.

[Act Five · Scene Four]

"As for the little Marquess, who sat squeezing my hand for such a long while yesterday, I find him in all respects the most trifling creature alive; and the only things of value about him are his cape and his sword. As for the man with the green ribbons . . ."

(*To Alceste*)
It's your turn now, Sir.

"As for the man with the green ribbons, he amuses me now and then with his bluntness and his bearish ill-humor; but there are many times indeed when I think him the greatest bore in the world. And as for the sonneteer . . ."

(*To Oronte*)
Here's your helping.

"And as for the sonneteer, who has taken it into his head to be witty, and insists on being an author in the teeth of opinion, I simply cannot be bothered to listen to him, and his prose wearies me quite as much as his poetry. Be assured that I am not always so well-entertained as you suppose; that I long for your company, more than I dare to say, at all these entertainments to which people drag me; and that the presence of those one loves is the true and perfect seasoning to all one's pleasures."

CLITANDRE

And now for me.

"Clitandre, whom you mention, and who so pesters me with his saccharine speeches, is the last man on earth for whom I could feel any affection. He is quite mad to

[*Act Five · Scene Four*]

suppose that I love him, and so are you, to doubt that
you are loved. Do come to your senses; exchange your
suppositions for his; and visit me as often as possible,
to help me bear the annoyance of his unwelcome attentions."

It's a sweet character that these letters show,
And what to call it, Madam, you well know.
Enough. We're off to make the world acquainted
With this sublime self-portrait that you've painted.

ACASTE

Madam, I'll make you no farewell oration;
No, you're not worthy of my indignation.
Far choicer hearts than yours, as you'll discover,
Would like this little Marquess for a lover.

SCENE FIVE

**CELIMENE, ELIANTE, ARSINOE, ALCESTE,
ORONTE, PHILINTE**

ORONTE

So! After all those loving letters you wrote,
You turn on me like this, and cut my throat!
And your dissembling, faithless heart, I find,
Has pledged itself by turns to all mankind!
How blind I've been! But now I clearly see;
I thank you, Madam, for enlightening me.
My heart is mine once more, and I'm content;
The loss of it shall be your punishment.
(*To Alceste*)
Sir, she is yours; I'll seek no more to stand
Between your wishes and this lady's hand.

SCENE SIX

CELIMENE, ELIANTE, ARSINOE, ALCESTE, PHILINTE

ARSINOE, *to Célimène*

Madam, I'm forced to speak. I'm far too stirred
To keep my counsel, after what I've heard.
I'm shocked and staggered by your want of morals.
It's not my way to mix in others' quarrels;
But really, when this fine and noble spirit,
This man of honor and surpassing merit,
Laid down the offering of his heart before you,
How *could* you . . .

ALCESTE

Madam, permit me, I implore you,
To represent myself in this debate.
Don't bother, please, to be my advocate.
My heart, in any case, could not afford
To give your services their due reward;
And if I chose, for consolation's sake,
Some other lady, t'would not be you I'd take.

[Act Five · Scene Six]

ARSINOE

What makes you think you could, Sir? And how dare
  you
Imply that I've been trying to ensnare you?
If you can for a moment entertain
Such flattering fancies, you're extremely vain.
I'm not so interested as you suppose
In Célimène's discarded gigolos.
Get rid of that absurd illusion, do.
Women like me are not for such as you.
Stay with this creature, to whom you're so attached;
I've never seen two people better matched.

SCENE SEVEN

CELIMENE, ELIANTE, ALCESTE, PHILINTE

ALCESTE, *to Célimène*

Well, I've been still throughout this exposé,
Till everyone but me has said his say.
Come, have I shown sufficient self-restraint?
And may I now . . .

CELIMENE

Yes, make your just complaint.
Reproach me freely, call me what you will;
You've every right to say I've used you ill.
I've wronged you, I confess it; and in my shame
I'll make no effort to escape the blame.
The anger of those others I could despise;
My guilt toward you I sadly recognize.
Your wrath is wholly justified, I fear;
I know how culpable I must appear,
I know all things bespeak my treachery,
And that, in short, you've grounds for hating me.
Do so; I give you leave.

[Act Five · Scene Seven]

ALCESTE

                Ah, traitress—how,
How should I cease to love you, even now?
Though mind and will were passionately bent
On hating you, my heart would not consent.
(*To Eliante and Philinte*)
Be witness to my madness, both of you;
See what infatuation drives one to;
But wait; my folly's only just begun,
And I shall prove to you before I'm done
How strange the human heart is, and how far
From rational we sorry creatures are.
(*To Célimène*)
Woman, I'm willing to forget your shame,
And clothe your treacheries in a sweeter name;
I'll call them youthful errors, instead of crimes,
And lay the blame on these corrupting times.
My one condition is that you agree
To share my chosen fate, and fly with me
To that wild, trackless, solitary place
In which I shall forget the human race.
Only by such a course can you atone
For those atrocious letters; by that alone
Can you remove my present horror of you,
And make it possible for me to love you.

CELIMENE

What! *I* renounce the world at my young age,
And die of boredom in some hermitage?

[*Act Five · Scene Seven*]

ALCESTE

Ah, if you really loved me as you ought,
You wouldn't give the world a moment's thought;
Must you have me, and all the world beside?

CELIMENE

Alas, at twenty one is terrified
Of solitude. I fear I lack the force
And depth of soul to take so stern a course.
But if my hand in marriage will content you,
Why, there's a plan which I might well consent to,
And . . .

ALCESTE

      No, I detest you now. I could excuse
Everything else, but since you thus refuse
To love me wholly, as a wife should do,
And see the world in me, as I in you,
Go! I reject your hand, and disenthrall
My heart from your enchantments, once for all.

SCENE EIGHT

ELIANTE, ALCESTE, PHILINTE

ALCESTE, *to Eliante*

Madam, your virtuous beauty has no peer;
Of all this world, you only are sincere;
I've long esteemed you highly, as you know;
Permit me ever to esteem you so,
And if I do not now request your hand,
Forgive me, Madam, and try to understand.
I feel unworthy of it; I sense that fate
Does not intend me for the married state,
That I should do you wrong by offering you
My shattered heart's unhappy residue,
And that in short . . .

ELIANTE

Your argument's well taken:
Nor need you fear that I shall feel forsaken.
Were I to offer him this hand of mine,
Your friend Philinte, I think, would not decline.

[*Act Five · Scene Eight*]

PHILINTE

Ah, Madam, that's my heart's most cherished goal,
For which I'd gladly give my life and soul.

ALCESTE, *to Eliante and Philinte*

May you be true to all you now profess,
And so deserve unending happiness.
Meanwhile, betrayed and wronged in everything,
I'll flee this bitter world where vice is king,
And seek some spot unpeopled and apart
Where I'll be free to have an honest heart.

PHILINTE

Come, Madam, let's do everything we can
To change the mind of this unhappy man.

TARTUFFE

Tartuffe

COMEDY IN FIVE ACTS, 1669

For my brother Lawrence

INTRODUCTION

There may be people who deny comedy the right to be serious, and think it improper for any but trivial themes to consort with laughter. It would take people of that kind to find in *Tartuffe* anything offensive to religion. The warped characters of the play express an obviously warped religious attitude, which is corrected by the reasonable orthodoxy of Cléante, the wholesomeness of Dorine, and the entire testimony of the action. The play is not a satire on religion, as those held who kept it off the boards for five years. Is it, then, a satire on religious hypocrisy, as Molière claimed in his polemical preface of 1669?

The play speaks often of religious hypocrisy, displays it in action, and sometimes seems to be gesturing toward its practitioners in seventeenth-century French society. Tartuffe is made to recommend, more than once, those Jesuitical techniques for easing the conscience which Pascal attacked in the *Provincial Letters*. Cléante makes a long speech against people who feign piety for the sake of preferment or political advantage. And yet no one in the play can be said to be a religious hypocrite in any representative sense. Tartuffe may at times suggest or symbolize the slippery casuist, or the sort of hypocrite denounced by Cléante, but he is not himself such a person. He is a versatile parasite or confidence man, with a very long criminal record, and to pose as a holy man is not his only *modus operandi:* we see him, in the last act, shifting easily from the role of saint to that of hundred-percenter. As for the other major characters who might qualify, Madame Pernelle is simply a nasty bigot, while the religious attitudes of her son Orgon are, for all their underlying corruption, quite sincere.

[*Introduction*]

Tartuffe is only incidentally satiric; what we experience in reading or seeing it, as several modern critics have argued, is not a satire but a "deep" comedy in which (1) a knave tries to control life by cold chicanery, (2) a fool tries to oppress life by unconscious misuse of the highest values, and (3) life, happily, will not have it.

Orgon, the central character of the play, is a rich bourgeois of middle age, with two grown children by his first wife. His second wife, Elmire, is attractive, young, and socially clever. We gather from the maid Dorine that Orgon has until lately seemed a good and sensible man, but the Orgon whom we meet in Act I, Scene 4 has become a fool. What has happened to him? It appears that he, like many another middle-aged man, has been alarmed by a sense of failing powers and failing authority, and that he has compensated by adopting an extreme religious severity. In this he is comparable to the aging coquette described by Dorine, who "quits a world which fast is quitting her," and saves face by becoming a censorious prude.

Orgon's resort to bigotry has coincided with his discovery of Tartuffe, a wily opportunist who imposes upon him by a pretense of sanctity, and is soon established in Orgon's house as honored guest, spiritual guide, and moral censor. Tartuffe's attitude toward Orgon is perfectly simple: he regards his benefactor as a dupe, and proposes to swindle him as badly as he can. Orgon's attitude toward Tartuffe is more complex and far less conscious. It consists, in part, of an unnatural fondness or "crush" about which the clear-sighted Dorine is explicit:

> *He pets and pampers him with love more tender*
> *Than any pretty mistress could engender....*

It also involves, in the strict sense of the word, idolatry: Orgon's febrile religious emotions are all related to Tartuffe

[Introduction]

and appear to terminate in him. Finally, and least consciously, Orgon cherishes Tartuffe because, with the sanction of the latter's austere precepts, he can tyrannize over his family and punish them for possessing what he feels himself to be losing: youth, gaiety, strong natural desires. This punitive motive comes to the surface, looking like plain sadism, when Orgon orders his daughter to

> *Marry Tartuffe, and mortify your flesh!*

Orgon is thus both Tartuffe's victim and his unconscious exploiter; once we apprehend this, we can better understand Orgon's stubborn refusal to see Tartuffe for the fraud that he is.

When Orgon says to Cléante,

> *My mother, children, brother and wife could die,*
> *And I'd not feel a single moment's pain,*

he is parodying or perverting a Christian idea which derives from the Gospels and rings out purely in Luther's "A Mighty Fortress is Our God":

> *Let goods and kindred go,*
> *This mortal life also....*

The trouble with Orgon's high spirituality is that one cannot obey the first commandment without obeying the second also. Orgon has withdrawn all proper feeling from those about him, and his vicious fatuity creates an atmosphere which is the comic equivalent of *King Lear*'s. All natural bonds of love and trust are strained or broken; evil is taken for good; truth must to kennel. Cléante's reasonings, the rebellious protests of Damis, the entreaties of Mariane, and the mockeries of Dorine are ineffectual against Orgon's folly; he must see Tartuffe paw at his wife, and hear Tartuffe speak contemptuously of him, before he is willing to part with the sponsor of his spiteful piety. How little "religion" there has been in Orgon's behavior, how much it has arisen from infatuation and bitterness, we may judge by his indiscriminate outburst in the fifth act:

> *Enough, by God! I'm through with pious men!*
> *Henceforth I'll hate the whole false brotherhood,*
> *And persecute them worse than Satan could.*

By the time Orgon is made to see Tartuffe's duplicity, the latter has accomplished his swindle, and is in a position to bring about Orgon's material ruin. It takes Louis XIV himself to save the day, in a conclusion which may seem both forced and flattering, but which serves to contrast a judicious, humane and forgiving ruler with the domestic tyrant Orgon. The King's moral insight is Tartuffe's final undoing; nevertheless there is an earlier scene in which we are given better assurance of the invincibility of the natural and sane. I refer to Tartuffe's first conversation with Elmire, in which passion compels the hypocrite recklessly to abandon his role. What comes out of Tartuffe in that scene is an expression of helpless lust, couched in an appalling mixture of the languages of gallantry and devotion. It is not attractive; and yet one is profoundly satisfied to discover that, as W. G. Moore puts it, "Tartuffe's human nature escapes his calculation." To be flawlessly monstrous is, thank heaven, not easy.

In translating *Tartuffe* I have tried, as with *The Misanthrope* some years ago, to reproduce with all possible fidelity both Molière's words and his poetic form. The necessity of keeping verse and rhyme, in such plays as these, was argued at some length in an introduction to the earlier translation, and I shall not repeat all those arguments here. It is true that *Tartuffe* presents an upper-bourgeois rather than a courtly milieu; there is less deliberate wit and ele-

[*Introduction*]

gance than in the dialogue of *The Misanthrope,* and consequently there is less call for the couplet as a conveyor of epigrammatic effects. Yet there are such effects in *Tartuffe,* and rhyme and verse are required here for other good reasons: to pay out the long speeches with clarifying emphasis, and at an assimilable rate; to couple farcical sequences to passages of greater weight and resonance; and to give a purely formal pleasure, as when balancing verse-patterns support the "ballet" movement of the close of Act II. My convictions being what they are, I am happy to report what a number of productions of the *Misanthrope* translation have shown: that contemporary audiences are quite willing to put up with rhymed verse on the stage.

I thank Messrs. Jacques Barzun and Eric Bentley for encouraging me to undertake this translation; Messrs. Harry Levin, Frederic Musser and Edward Williamson for suggesting improvements in the text; and the Ford and Philadelphia Community Foundations for their support of the project.

Richard Wilbur

Portland, Connecticut
February, 1963

CHARACTERS

MME PERNELLE, Orgon's mother
ORGON, Elmire's husband
ELMIRE, Orgon's wife
DAMIS, Orgon's son, Elmire's stepson
MARIANE, Orgon's daughter, Elmire's stepdaughter, in love with Valère
VALÈRE, in love with Mariane
CLÉANTE, Orgon's brother-in-law
TARTUFFE, a hypocrite
DORINE, Mariane's lady's-maid
M. LOYAL, a bailiff
A POLICE OFFICER
FLIPOTE, Mme Pernelle's maid

The scene throughout: Orgon's house in Paris

Act 1

SCENE ONE

MADAME PERNELLE *and* FLIPOTE, *her maid,* ELMIRE, MARIANE, DORINE, DAMIS, CLÉANTE

MADAME PERNELLE

Come, come, Flipote; it's time I left this place.

ELMIRE

I can't keep up, you walk at such a pace.

MADAME PERNELLE

Don't trouble, child; no need to show me out.
It's not your manners I'm concerned about.

ELMIRE

We merely pay you the respect we owe.
But, Mother, why this hurry? Must you go?

MADAME PERNELLE

I must. This house appals me. No one in it
Will pay attention for a single minute.

[Act One · Scene One]

Children, I take my leave much vexed in spirit.
I offer good advice, but you won't hear it.
You all break in and chatter on and on.
It's like a madhouse with the keeper gone.

DORINE

If . . .

MADAME PERNELLE

Girl, you talk too much, and I'm afraid
You're far too saucy for a lady's-maid.
You push in everywhere and have your say.

DAMIS

But . . .

MADAME PERNELLE

You, boy, grow more foolish every day.
To think my grandson should be such a dunce!
I've said a hundred times, if I've said it once,
That if you keep the course on which you've started,
You'll leave your worthy father broken-hearted.

MARIANE

I think . . .

[Act One · Scene One]

MADAME PERNELLE

And you, his sister, seem so pure,
So shy, so innocent, and so demure.
But you know what they say about still waters.
I pity parents with secretive daughters.

ELMIRE

Now, Mother...

MADAME PERNELLE

And as for you, child, let me add
That your behavior is extremely bad,
And a poor example for these children, too.
Their dear, dead mother did far better than you.
You're much too free with money, and I'm distressed
To see you so elaborately dressed.
When it's one's husband that one aims to please,
One has no need of costly fripperies.

CLÉANTE

Oh, Madam, really...

MADAME PERNELLE

You are her brother, Sir,
And I respect and love you; yet if I were
My son, this lady's good and pious spouse,
I wouldn't make you welcome in my house.

[Act One · Scene One]

You're full of worldly counsels which, I fear,
Aren't suitable for decent folk to hear.
I've spoken bluntly, Sir; but it behooves us
Not to mince words when righteous fervor moves us.

DAMIS

Your man Tartuffe is full of holy speeches...

MADAME PERNELLE

And practises precisely what he preaches.
He's a fine man, and should be listened to.
I will not hear him mocked by fools like you.

DAMIS

Good God! Do you expect me to submit
To the tyranny of that carping hypocrite?
Must we forgo all joys and satisfactions
Because that bigot censures all our actions?

DORINE

To hear him talk—and he talks all the time—
There's nothing one can do that's not a crime.
He rails at everything, your dear Tartuffe.

MADAME PERNELLE

Whatever he reproves deserves reproof.
He's out to save your souls, and all of you
Must love him, as my son would have you do.

[Act One · Scene One]

DAMIS

Ah no, Grandmother, I could never take
To such a rascal, even for my father's sake.
That's how I feel, and I shall not dissemble.
His every action makes me seethe and tremble
With helpless anger, and I have no doubt
That he and I will shortly have it out.

DORINE

Surely it is a shame and a disgrace
To see this man usurp the master's place—
To see this beggar who, when first he came,
Had not a shoe or shoestring to his name
So far forget himself that he behaves
As if the house were his, and we his slaves.

MADAME PERNELLE

Well, mark my words, your souls would fare far better
If you obeyed his precepts to the letter.

DORINE

You see him as a saint. I'm far less awed;
In fact, I see right through him. He's a fraud.

MADAME PERNELLE

Nonsense!

[*Act One* · *Scene One*]

DORINE

      His man Laurent's the same, or worse;
I'd not trust either with a penny purse.

MADAME PERNELLE

I can't say what his servant's morals may be;
His own great goodness I can guarantee.
You all regard him with distaste and fear
Because he tells you what you're loath to hear,
Condemns your sins, points out your moral flaws,
And humbly strives to further Heaven's cause.

DORINE

If sin is all that bothers him, why is it
He's so upset when folk drop in to visit?
Is Heaven so outraged by a social call
That he must prophesy against us all?
I'll tell you what I think: if you ask me,
He's jealous of my mistress' company.

MADAME PERNELLE

Rubbish! (*To Elmire:*) He's not alone, child, in complaining
Of all of your promiscuous entertaining.
Why, the whole neighborhood's upset, I know,
By all these carriages that come and go,

[*Act One · Scene One*]

With crowds of guests parading in and out
And noisy servants loitering about.
In all of this, I'm sure there's nothing vicious;
But why give people cause to be suspicious?

CLÉANTE

They need no cause; they'll talk in any case.
Madam, this world would be a joyless place
If, fearing what malicious tongues might say,
We locked our doors and turned our friends away.
And even if one did so dreary a thing,
D'you think those tongues would cease their chattering?
One can't fight slander; it's a losing battle;
Let us instead ignore their tittle-tattle.
Let's strive to live by conscience' clear decrees,
And let the gossips gossip as they please.

DORINE

If there is talk against us, I know the source:
It's Daphne and her little husband, of course.
Those who have greatest cause for guilt and shame
Are quickest to besmirch a neighbor's name.
When there's a chance for libel, they never miss it;
When something can be made to seem illicit
They're off at once to spread the joyous news,
Adding to fact what fantasies they choose.
By talking up their neighbor's indiscretions
They seek to camouflage their own transgressions,

[*Act One · Scene One*]

Hoping that others' innocent affairs
Will lend a hue of innocence to theirs,
Or that their own black guilt will come to seem
Part of a general shady color-scheme.

MADAME PERNELLE

All that is quite irrelevant. I doubt
That anyone's more virtuous and devout
Than dear Orante; and I'm informed that she
Condemns your mode of life most vehemently.

DORINE

Oh, yes, she's strict, devout, and has no taint
Of worldliness; in short, she seems a saint.
But it was time which taught her that disguise;
She's thus because she can't be otherwise.
So long as her attractions could enthrall,
She flounced and flirted and enjoyed it all,
But now that they're no longer what they were
She quits a world which fast is quitting her,
And wears a veil of virtue to conceal
Her bankrupt beauty and her lost appeal.
That's what becomes of old coquettes today:
Distressed when all their lovers fall away,
They see no recourse but to play the prude,
And so confer a style on solitude.
Thereafter, they're severe with everyone,
Condemning all our actions, pardoning none,

[Act One · Scene One]

And claiming to be pure, austere, and zealous
When, if the truth were known, they're merely jealous,
And cannot bear to see another know
The pleasures time has forced them to forgo.

MADAME PERNELLE (*Initially to Elmire:*)

That sort of talk is what you like to hear;
Therefore you'd have us all keep still, my dear,
While Madam rattles on the livelong day.
Nevertheless, I mean to have my say.
I tell you that you're blest to have Tartuffe
Dwelling, as my son's guest, beneath this roof;
That Heaven has sent him to forestall its wrath
By leading you, once more, to the true path;
That all he reprehends is reprehensible,
And that you'd better heed him, and be sensible.
These visits, balls, and parties in which you revel
Are nothing but inventions of the Devil.
One never hears a word that's edifying:
Nothing but chaff and foolishness and lying,
As well as vicious gossip in which one's neighbor
Is cut to bits with epee, foil, and saber.
People of sense are driven half-insane
At such affairs, where noise and folly reign
And reputations perish thick and fast.
As a wise preacher said on Sunday last,
Parties are Towers of Babylon, because
The guests all babble on with never a pause;
And then he told a story which, I think...
        (*To Cléante:*)
I heard that laugh, Sir, and I saw that wink!

[Act One · Scene One]

Go find your silly friends and laugh some more!
Enough; I'm going; don't show me to the door.
I leave this household much dismayed and vexed;
I cannot say when I shall see you next.
                (Slapping Flipote:)
Wake up, don't stand there gaping into space!
I'll slap some sense into that stupid face.
Move, move, you slut.

SCENE TWO

CLÉANTE, DORINE

CLÉANTE

                I think I'll stay behind;
I want no further pieces of her mind.
How that old lady...

DORINE

                Oh, what wouldn't she say
If she could hear you speak of her that way!
She'd thank you for the *lady*, but I'm sure
She'd find the *old* a little premature.

CLÉANTE

My, what a scene she made, and what a din!
And how this man Tartuffe has taken her in!

DORINE

Yes, but her son is even worse deceived;
His folly must be seen to be believed.

[*Act One · Scene Two*]

In the late troubles, he played an able part
And served his king with wise and loyal heart,
But he's quite lost his senses since he fell
Beneath Tartuffe's infatuating spell.
He calls him brother, and loves him as his life,
Preferring him to mother, child, or wife.
In him and him alone will he confide;
He's made him his confessor and his guide;
He pets and pampers him with love more tender
Than any pretty mistress could engender,
Gives him the place of honor when they dine,
Delights to see him gorging like a swine,
Stuffs him with dainties till his guts distend,
And when he belches, cries "God bless you, friend!"
In short, he's mad; he worships him; he dotes;
His deeds he marvels at, his words he quotes,
Thinking each act a miracle, each word
Oracular as those that Moses heard.
Tartuffe, much pleased to find so easy a victim,
Has in a hundred ways beguiled and tricked him,
Milked him of money, and with his permission
Established here a sort of Inquisition.
Even Laurent, his lackey, dares to give
Us arrogant advice on how to live;
He sermonizes us in thundering tones
And confiscates our ribbons and colognes.
Last week he tore a kerchief into pieces
Because he found it pressed in a *Life of Jesus:*
He said it was a sin to juxtapose
Unholy vanities and holy prose.

SCENE THREE

ELMIRE, MARIANE, DAMIS, CLÉANTE, DORINE

ELMIRE (*To Cléante:*)

You did well not to follow; she stood in the door
And said *verbatim* all she'd said before.
I saw my husband coming. I think I'd best
Go upstairs now, and take a little rest.

CLÉANTE

I'll wait and greet him here; then I must go.
I've really only time to say hello.

DAMIS

Sound him about my sister's wedding, please.
I think Tartuffe's against it, and that he's
Been urging Father to withdraw his blessing.
As you well know, I'd find that most distressing.
Unless my sister and Valère can marry,
My hopes to wed *his* sister will miscarry,
And I'm determined . . .

DORINE

He's coming.

SCENE FOUR

ORGON, CLÉANTE, DORINE

ORGON

Ah, Brother, good-day.

CLÉANTE

Well, welcome back. I'm sorry I can't stay.
How was the country? Blooming, I trust, and green?

ORGON

Excuse me, Brother; just one moment.
(*To Dorine:*)
Dorine...
(*To Cléante:*)
To put my mind at rest, I always learn
The household news the moment I return.
(*To Dorine:*)
Has all been well, these two days I've been gone?
How are the family? What's been going on?

[Act One · Scene Four]

DORINE

Your wife, two days ago, had a bad fever,
And a fierce headache which refused to leave her.

ORGON

Ah. And Tartuffe?

DORINE

Tartuffe? Why, he's round and red,
Bursting with health, and excellently fed.

ORGON

Poor fellow!

DORINE

That night, the mistress was unable
To take a single bite at the dinner-table.
Her headache-pains, she said, were simply hellish.

ORGON

Ah. And Tartuffe?

[*Act One · Scene Four*]

DORINE

>He ate his meal with relish,
And zealously devoured in her presence
A leg of mutton and a brace of pheasants.

ORGON

Poor fellow!

DORINE

>Well, the pains continued strong,
And so she tossed and tossed the whole night long,
Now icy-cold, now burning like a flame.
We sat beside her bed till morning came.

ORGON

Ah. And Tartuffe?

DORINE

>Why, having eaten, he rose
And sought his room, already in a doze,
Got into his warm bed, and snored away
In perfect peace until the break of day.

ORGON

Poor fellow!

[*Act One · Scene Four*]

DORINE

   After much ado, we talked her
Into dispatching someone for the doctor.
He bled her, and the fever quickly fell.

ORGON

Ah. And Tartuffe?

DORINE

    He bore it very well.
To keep his cheerfulness at any cost,
And make up for the blood *Madame* had lost,
He drank, at lunch, four beakers full of port.

ORGON

Poor fellow!

DORINE

   Both are doing well, in short.
I'll go and tell *Madame* that you've expressed
Keen sympathy and anxious interest.

SCENE FIVE

ORGON, CLÉANTE

CLÉANTE

That girl was laughing in your face, and though
I've no wish to offend you, even so
I'm bound to say that she had some excuse.
How can you possibly be such a goose?
Are you so dazed by this man's hocus-pocus
That all the world, save him, is out of focus?
You've given him clothing, shelter, food, and care;
Why must you also . . .

ORGON

              Brother, stop right there.
You do not know the man of whom you speak.

CLÉANTE

I grant you that. But my judgment's not so weak
That I can't tell, by his effect on others . . .

[Act One · Scene Five]

ORGON

Ah, when you meet him, you two will be like brothers!
There's been no loftier soul since time began.
He is a man who... a man who... an excellent man.
To keep his precepts is to be reborn,
And view this dunghill of a world with scorn.
Yes, thanks to him I'm a changed man indeed.
Under his tutelage my soul's been freed
From earthly loves, and every human tie:
My mother, children, brother, and wife could die,
And I'd not feel a single moment's pain.

CLÉANTE

That's a fine sentiment, Brother; most humane.

ORGON

Oh, had you seen Tartuffe as I first knew him,
Your heart, like mine, would have surrendered to him.
He used to come into our church each day
And humbly kneel nearby, and start to pray.
He'd draw the eyes of everybody there
By the deep fervor of his heartfelt prayer;
He'd sigh and weep, and sometimes with a sound
Of rapture he would bend and kiss the ground;
And when I rose to go, he'd run before
To offer me holy-water at the door.
His serving-man, no less devout than he,
Informed me of his master's poverty;

[*Act One · Scene Five*]

I gave him gifts, but in his humbleness
He'd beg me every time to give him less.
"Oh, that's too much," he'd cry, "too much by twice!
I don't deserve it. The half, Sir, would suffice."
And when I wouldn't take it back, he'd share
Half of it with the poor, right then and there.
At length, Heaven prompted me to take him in
To dwell with us, and free our souls from sin.
He guides our lives, and to protect my honor
Stays by my wife, and keeps an eye upon her;
He tells me whom she sees, and all she does,
And seems more jealous than I ever was!
And how austere he is! Why, he can detect
A mortal sin where you would least suspect;
In smallest trifles, he's extremely strict.
Last week, his conscience was severely pricked
Because, while praying, he had caught a flea
And killed it, so he felt, too wrathfully.

CLÉANTE

Good God, man! Have you lost your common sense—
Or is this all some joke at my expense?
How can you stand there and in all sobriety ...

ORGON

Brother, your language savors of impiety.
Too much free-thinking's made your faith unsteady,
And as I've warned you many times already,
'Twill get you into trouble before you're through.

[*Act One · Scene Five*]

CLÉANTE

So I've been told before by dupes like you:
Being blind, you'd have all others blind as well;
The clear-eyed man you call an infidel,
And he who sees through humbug and pretense
Is charged, by you, with want of reverence.
Spare me your warnings, Brother; I have no fear
Of speaking out, for you and Heaven to hear,
Against affected zeal and pious knavery.
There's true and false in piety, as in bravery,
And just as those whose courage shines the most
In battle, are the least inclined to boast,
So those whose hearts are truly pure and lowly
Don't make a flashy show of being holy.
There's a vast difference, so it seems to me,
Between true piety and hypocrisy:
How do you fail to see it, may I ask?
Is not a face quite different from a mask?
Cannot sincerity and cunning art,
Reality and semblance, be told apart?
Are scarecrows just like men, and do you hold
That a false coin is just as good as gold?
Ah, Brother, man's a strangely fashioned creature
Who seldom is content to follow Nature,
But recklessly pursues his inclination
Beyond the narrow bounds of moderation,
And often, by transgressing Reason's laws,
Perverts a lofty aim or noble cause.
A passing observation, but it applies.

[*Act One · Scene Five*]

ORGON

I see, dear Brother, that you're profoundly wise;
You harbor all the insight of the age.
You are our one clear mind, our only sage,
The era's oracle, its Cato too,
And all mankind are fools compared to you.

CLÉANTE

Brother, I don't pretend to be a sage,
Nor have I all the wisdom of the age.
There's just one insight I would dare to claim:
I know that true and false are not the same;
And just as there is nothing I more revere
Than a soul whose faith is steadfast and sincere,
Nothing that I more cherish and admire
Than honest zeal and true religious fire,
So there is nothing that I find more base
Than specious piety's dishonest face—
Than these bold mountebanks, these histrios
Whose impious mummeries and hollow shows
Exploit our love of Heaven, and make a jest
Of all that men think holiest and best;
These calculating souls who offer prayers
Not to their Maker, but as public wares,
And seek to buy respect and reputation
With lifted eyes and sighs of exaltation;
These charlatans, I say, whose pilgrim souls
Proceed, by way of Heaven, toward earthly goals,
Who weep and pray and swindle and extort,

[*Act One · Scene Five*]

Who preach the monkish life, but haunt the court,
Who make their zeal the partner of their vice—
Such men are vengeful, sly, and cold as ice,
And when there is an enemy to defame
They cloak their spite in fair religion's name,
Their private spleen and malice being made
To seem a high and virtuous crusade,
Until, to mankind's reverent applause,
They crucify their foe in Heaven's cause.
Such knaves are all too common; yet, for the wise,
True piety isn't hard to recognize,
And, happily, these present times provide us
With bright examples to instruct and guide us.
Consider Ariston and Périandre;
Look at Oronte, Alcidamas, Clitandre;
Their virtue is acknowledged; who could doubt it?
But you won't hear them beat the drum about it.
They're never ostentatious, never vain,
And their religion's moderate and humane;
It's not their way to criticize and chide:
They think censoriousness a mark of pride,
And therefore, letting others preach and rave,
They show, by deeds, how Christians should behave.
They think no evil of their fellow man,
But judge of him as kindly as they can.
They don't intrigue and wangle and conspire;
To lead a good life is their one desire;
The sinner wakes no rancorous hate in them;
It is the sin alone which they condemn;
Nor do they try to show a fiercer zeal
For Heaven's cause than Heaven itself could feel.
These men I honor, these men I advocate

[*Act One · Scene Five*]

As models for us all to emulate.
Your man is not their sort at all, I fear:
And, while your praise of him is quite sincere,
I think that you've been dreadfully deluded.

ORGON

Now then, dear Brother, is your speech concluded?

CLÉANTE

Why, yes.

ORGON

Your servant, Sir. (*He turns to go.*)

CLÉANTE

No, Brother; wait.
There's one more matter. You agreed of late
That young Valère might have your daughter's hand.

ORGON

I did.

CLÉANTE

And set the date, I understand.

[*Act One · Scene Five*]

ORGON

Quite so.

CLÉANTE

You've now postponed it; is that true?

ORGON

No doubt.

CLÉANTE

The match no longer pleases you?

ORGON

Who knows?

CLÉANTE

D'you mean to go back on your word?

ORGON

I won't say that.

CLÉANTE

Has anything occurred
Which might entitle you to break your pledge?

[*Act One · Scene Five*]

ORGON

Perhaps.

CLÉANTE

Why must you hem, and haw, and hedge?
The boy asked me to sound you in this affair...

ORGON

It's been a pleasure.

CLÉANTE

But what shall I tell Valère?

ORGON

Whatever you like.

CLÉANTE

But what have you decided?
What are your plans?

ORGON

I plan, Sir, to be guided
By Heaven's will.

[*Act One · Scene Five*]

CLÉANTE

Come, Brother, don't talk rot.
You've given Valère your word; will you keep it, or not?

ORGON

Good day.

CLÉANTE

This looks like poor Valère's undoing;
I'll go and warn him that there's trouble brewing.

Act 2

SCENE ONE

ORGON, MARIANE

ORGON

Mariane.

MARIANE

Yes, Father?

ORGON

A word with you; come here.

MARIANE

What are you looking for?

ORGON (*Peering into a small closet:*)

Eavesdroppers, dear.
I'm making sure we shan't be overheard.
Someone in there could catch our every word.
Ah, good, we're safe. Now, Mariane, my child,
You're a sweet girl who's tractable and mild,
Whom I hold dear, and think most highly of.

[Act Two · Scene One]

MARIANE

I'm deeply grateful, Father, for your love.

ORGON

That's well said, Daughter; and you can repay me
If, in all things, you'll cheerfully obey me.

MARIANE

To please you, Sir, is what delights me best.

ORGON

Good, good. Now, what d'you think of Tartuffe, our
 guest?

MARIANE

I, Sir?

ORGON

Yes. Weigh your answer; think it through.

MARIANE

Oh, dear. I'll say whatever you wish me to.

[Act Two · Scene One]

ORGON

That's wisely said, my Daughter. Say of him, then,
That he's the very worthiest of men,
And that you're fond of him, and would rejoice
In being his wife, if that should be my choice.
Well?

MARIANE

What?

ORGON

What's that?

MARIANE

I . . .

ORGON

Well?

MARIANE

Forgive me, pray.

ORGON

Did you not hear me?

[Act Two · Scene One]

MARIANE

Of *whom*, Sir, must I say
That I am fond of him, and would rejoice
In being his wife, if that should be your choice?

ORGON

Why, of Tartuffe.

MARIANE

But, Father, that's false, you know.
Why would you have me say what isn't so?

ORGON

Because I am resolved it shall be true.
That it's my wish should be enough for you.

MARIANE

You can't mean, Father . . .

ORGON

Yes, Tartuffe shall be
Allied by marriage to this family,
And he's to be your husband, is that clear?
It's a father's privilege . . .

SCENE TWO

DORINE, ORGON, MARIANE

ORGON (*To Dorine:*)

What are you doing in here?
Is curiosity so fierce a passion
With you, that you must eavesdrop in this fashion?

DORINE

There's lately been a rumor going about—
Based on some hunch or chance remark, no doubt—
That you mean Mariane to wed Tartuffe.
I've laughed it off, of course, as just a spoof.

ORGON

You find it so incredible?

DORINE

Yes, I do.
I won't accept that story, even from you.

[*Act Two · Scene Two*]

ORGON

Well, you'll believe it when the thing is done.

DORINE

Yes, yes, of course. Go on and have your fun.

ORGON

I've never been more serious in my life.

DORINE

Ha!

ORGON

Daughter, I mean it; you're to be his wife.

DORINE

No, don't believe your father; it's all a hoax.

ORGON

See here, young woman...

DORINE

Come, Sir, no more jokes;
You can't fool us.

[Act Two · Scene Two]

ORGON

    How dare you talk that way?

DORINE

All right, then: we believe you, sad to say.
But how a man like you, who looks so wise
And wears a moustache of such splendid size,
Can be so foolish as to . . .

ORGON

        Silence, please!
My girl, you take too many liberties.
I'm master here, as you must not forget.

DORINE

Do let's discuss this calmly; don't be upset.
You can't be serious, Sir, about this plan.
What should that bigot want with Mariane?
Praying and fasting ought to keep him busy.
And then, in terms of wealth and rank, what is he?
Why should a man of property like you
Pick out a beggar son-in-law?

ORGON

        That will do.
Speak of his poverty with reverence.
His is a pure and saintly indigence

[*Act Two · Scene Two*]

Which far transcends all worldly pride and pelf.
He lost his fortune, as he says himself,
Because he cared for Heaven alone, and so
Was careless of his interests here below.
I mean to get him out of his present straits
And help him to recover his estates—
Which, in his part of the world, have no small fame.
Poor though he is, he's a gentleman just the same.

DORINE

Yes, so he tells us; and, Sir, it seems to me
Such pride goes very ill with piety.
A man whose spirit spurns this dungy earth
Ought not to brag of lands and noble birth;
Such worldly arrogance will hardly square
With meek devotion and the life of prayer.
. . . But this approach, I see, has drawn a blank;
Let's speak, then, of his person, not his rank.
Doesn't it seem to you a trifle grim
To give a girl like her to a man like him?
When two are so ill-suited, can't you see
What the sad consequence is bound to be?
A young girl's virtue is imperilled, Sir,
When such a marriage is imposed on her;
For if one's bridegroom isn't to one's taste,
It's hardly an inducement to be chaste,
And many a man with horns upon his brow
Has made his wife the thing that she is now.
It's hard to be a faithful wife, in short,
To certain husbands of a certain sort,

[Act Two · Scene Two]

And he who gives his daughter to a man she hates
Must answer for her sins at Heaven's gates.
Think, Sir, before you play so risky a role.

ORGON

This servant-girl presumes to save my soul!

DORINE

You would do well to ponder what I've said.

ORGON

Daughter, we'll disregard this dunderhead.
Just trust your father's judgment. Oh, I'm aware
That I once promised you to young Valère;
But now I hear he gambles, which greatly shocks me;
What's more, I've doubts about his orthodoxy.
His visits to church, I note, are very few.

DORINE

Would you have him go at the same hours as you,
And kneel nearby, to be sure of being seen?

ORGON

I can dispense with such remarks, Dorine.
               (*To Mariane:*)
Tartuffe, however, is sure of Heaven's blessing,
And that's the only treasure worth possessing.

[Act Two · Scene Two]

This match will bring you joys beyond all measure;
Your cup will overflow with every pleasure;
You two will interchange your faithful loves
Like two sweet cherubs, or two turtle-doves.
No harsh word shall be heard, no frown be seen,
And he shall make you happy as a queen.

DORINE

And she'll make him a cuckold, just wait and see.

ORGON

What language!

DORINE

         Oh, he's a man of destiny;
He's *made* for horns, and what the stars demand
Your daughter's virtue surely can't withstand.

ORGON

Don't interrupt me further. Why can't you learn
That certain things are none of your concern?

DORINE

It's for your own sake that I interfere.
    (She repeatedly interrupts Orgon just as he is turning to speak to his daughter:)

[*Act Two · Scene Two*]

ORGON

Most kind of you. Now, hold your tongue, d'you hear?

DORINE

If I didn't love you...

ORGON

Spare me your affection.

DORINE

I'll love you, Sir, in spite of your objection.

ORGON

Blast!

DORINE

I can't bear, Sir, for your honor's sake,
To let you make this ludicrous mistake.

ORGON

You mean to go on talking?

DORINE

If I didn't protest
This sinful marriage, my conscience couldn't rest.

[*Act Two · Scene Two*]

ORGON

If you don't hold your tongue, you little shrew...

DORINE

What, lost your temper? A pious man like you?

ORGON

Yes! Yes! You talk and talk. I'm maddened by it.
Once and for all, I tell you to be quiet.

DORINE

Well, I'll be quiet. But I'll be thinking hard.

ORGON

Think all you like, but you had better guard
That saucy tongue of yours, or I'll...
   (*Turning back to Mariane:*)
         Now, child,
I've weighed this matter fully.

DORINE (*Aside:*)
        It drives me wild
That I can't speak.
  (*Orgon turns his head, and she is silent.*)

[Act Two · Scene Two]

ORGON

        Tartuffe is no young dandy,
But, still, his person . . .

DORINE (*Aside:*)

        Is as sweet as candy.

ORGON

Is such that, even if you shouldn't care
For his other merits . . .
    (*He turns and stands facing Dorine, arms crossed.*)

DORINE (*Aside:*)

        They'll make a lovely pair.
If I were she, no man would marry me
Against my inclination, and go scot-free.
He'd learn, before the wedding-day was over,
How readily a wife can find a lover.

ORGON (*To Dorine:*)

It seems you treat my orders as a joke.

DORINE

Why, what's the matter? 'Twas not to you I spoke.

[Act Two · Scene Two]

ORGON

What *were* you doing?

DORINE

Talking to myself, that's all.

ORGON

Ah! (*Aside:*) One more bit of impudence and gall,
And I shall give her a good slap in the face.
  (*He puts himself in position to slap her; Dorine, whenever he glances at her, stands immobile and silent:*)
Daughter, you shall accept, and with good grace,
The husband I've selected... Your wedding-day...
  (*To Dorine:*)
Why don't you talk to yourself?

DORINE

I've nothing to say.

ORGON

Come, just one word.

DORINE

No thank you, Sir. I pass.

[Act Two · Scene Two]

ORGON

Come, speak; I'm waiting.

DORINE

                I'd not be such an ass.

ORGON (*Turning to Mariane:*)

In short, dear Daughter, I mean to be obeyed,
And you must bow to the sound choice I've made.

DORINE (*Moving away:*)

I'd not wed such a monster, even in jest.
        (*Orgon attempts to slap her, but misses.*)

ORGON

Daughter, that maid of yours is a thorough pest;
She makes me sinfully annoyed and nettled.
I can't speak further; my nerves are too unsettled.
She's so upset me by her insolent talk,
I'll calm myself by going for a walk.

SCENE THREE

DORINE, MARIANE

DORINE (*Returning:*)

Well, have you lost your tongue, girl? Must I play
Your part, and say the lines you ought to say?
Faced with a fate so hideous and absurd,
Can you not utter one dissenting word?

MARIANE

What good would it do? A father's power is great.

DORINE

Resist him now, or it will be too late.

MARIANE

But...

DORINE

Tell him one cannot love at a father's whim;
That you shall marry for yourself, not him;

[*Act Two · Scene Three*]

That since it's you who are to be the bride,
It's you, not he, who must be satisfied;
And that if his Tartuffe is so sublime,
He's free to marry him at any time.

MARIANE

I've bowed so long to Father's strict control,
I couldn't oppose him now, to save my soul.

DORINE

Come, come, Mariane. Do listen to reason, won't you?
Valère has asked your hand. Do you love him, or don't
 you?

MARIANE

Oh, how unjust of you! What can you mean
By asking such a question, dear Dorine?
You know the depth of my affection for him;
I've told you a hundred times how I adore him.

DORINE

I don't believe in everything I hear;
Who knows if your professions were sincere?

MARIANE

They were, Dorine, and you do me wrong to doubt it;
Heaven knows that I've been all too frank about it.

[Act Two · Scene Three]

DORINE

You love him, then?

MARIANE

Oh, more than I can express.

DORINE

And he, I take it, cares for you no less?

MARIANE

I think so.

DORINE

And you both, with equal fire,
Burn to be married?

MARIANE

That is our one desire.

DORINE

What of Tartuffe, then? What of your father's plan?

MARIANE

I'll kill myself, if I'm forced to wed that man.

[*Act Two · Scene Three*]

DORINE

I hadn't thought of that recourse. How splendid!
Just die, and all your troubles will be ended!
A fine solution. Oh, it maddens me
To hear you talk in that self-pitying key.

MARIANE

Dorine, how harsh you are! It's most unfair.
You have no sympathy for my despair.

DORINE

I've none at all for people who talk drivel
And, faced with difficulties, whine and snivel.

MARIANE

No doubt I'm timid, but it would be wrong...

DORINE

True love requires a heart that's firm and strong.

MARIANE

I'm strong in my affection for Valère,
But coping with my father is his affair.

[*Act Two · Scene Three*]

DORINE

But if your father's brain has grown so cracked
Over his dear Tartuffe that he can retract
His blessing, though your wedding-day was named,
It's surely not Valère who's to be blamed.

MARIANE

If I defied my father, as you suggest,
Would it not seem unmaidenly, at best?
Shall I defend my love at the expense
Of brazenness and disobedience?
Shall I parade my heart's desires, and flaunt . . .

DORINE

No, I ask nothing of you. Clearly you want
To be Madame Tartuffe, and I feel bound
Not to oppose a wish so very sound.
What right have I to criticize the match?
Indeed, my dear, the man's a brilliant catch.
Monsieur Tartuffe! Now, there's a man of weight!
Yes, yes, Monsieur Tartuffe, I'm bound to state,
Is quite a person; that's not to be denied;
'Twill be no little thing to be his bride.
The world already rings with his renown;
He's a great noble—in his native town;
His ears are red, he has a pink complexion,
And all in all, he'll suit you to perfection.

[Act Two · Scene Three]

MARIANE

Dear God!

DORINE

      Oh, how triumphant you will feel
At having caught a husband so ideal!

MARIANE

Oh, do stop teasing, and use your cleverness
To get me out of this appalling mess.
Advise me, and I'll do whatever you say.

DORINE

Ah no, a dutiful daughter must obey
Her father, even if he weds her to an ape.
You've a bright future; why struggle to escape?
Tartuffe will take you back where his family lives,
To a small town aswarm with relatives—
Uncles and cousins whom you'll be charmed to meet.
You'll be received at once by the elite,
Calling upon the bailiff's wife, no less—
Even, perhaps, upon the mayoress,
Who'll sit you down in the *best* kitchen chair.
Then, once a year, you'll dance at the village fair
To the drone of bagpipes—two of them, in fact—
And see a puppet-show, or an animal act.
Your husband...

[*Act Two · Scene Three*]

MARIANE

Oh, you turn my blood to ice!
Stop torturing me, and give me your advice.

DORINE (*Threatening to go:*)

Your servant, Madam.

MARIANE

Dorine, I beg of you . . .

DORINE

No, you deserve it; this marriage must go through.

MARIANE

Dorine!

DORINE

No.

MARIANE

Not Tartuffe! You know I think him . . .

DORINE

Tartuffe's your cup of tea, and you shall drink him.

[Act Two · Scene Three]

MARIANE

I've always told you everything, and relied...

DORINE

No. You deserve to be tartuffified.

MARIANE

Well, since you mock me and refuse to care,
I'll henceforth seek my solace in despair:
Despair shall be my counsellor and friend,
And help me bring my sorrows to an end.
(She starts to leave.)

DORINE

There now, come back; my anger has subsided.
You do deserve some pity, I've decided.

MARIANE

Dorine, if Father makes me undergo
This dreadful martyrdom, I'll die, I know.

DORINE

Don't fret; it won't be difficult to discover
Some plan of action... But here's Valère, your lover.

SCENE FOUR

VALÈRE, MARIANE, DORINE

VALÈRE

Madam, I've just received some wondrous news
Regarding which I'd like to hear your views.

MARIANE

What news?

VALÈRE

        You're marrying Tartuffe.

MARIANE

                        I find
That Father does have such a match in mind.

VALÈRE

Your father, Madam . . .

[*Act Two · Scene Four*]

MARIANE

. . . has just this minute said
That it's Tartuffe he wishes me to wed.

VALÈRE

Can he be serious?

MARIANE

Oh, indeed he can;
He's clearly set his heart upon the plan.

VALÈRE

And what position do you propose to take,
Madam?

MARIANE

Why—I don't know.

VALÈRE

For heaven's sake—
You don't know?

MARIANE

No.

[*Act Two · Scene Four*]

VALÈRE

Well, well!

MARIANE

Advise me, do.

VALÈRE

Marry the man. That's my advice to you.

MARIANE

That's your advice?

VALÈRE

Yes.

MARIANE

Truly?

VALÈRE

Oh, absolutely.
You couldn't choose more wisely, more astutely.

MARIANE

Thanks for this counsel; I'll follow it, of course.

[Act Two · Scene Four]

VALÈRE

Do, do; I'm sure 'twill cost you no remorse.

MARIANE

To give it didn't cause your heart to break.

VALÈRE

I gave it, Madam, only for your sake.

MARIANE

And it's for your sake that I take it, Sir.

DORINE (*Withdrawing to the rear of the stage:*)

Let's see which fool will prove the stubborner.

VALÈRE

So! I am nothing to you, and it was flat
Deception when you ...

MARIANE

           Please, enough of that.
You've told me plainly that I should agree
To wed the man my father's chosen for me,
And since you've deigned to counsel me so wisely,
I promise, Sir, to do as you advise me.

[*Act Two · Scene Four*]

VALÈRE

Ah, no, 'twas not by me that you were swayed.
No, your decision was already made;
Though now, to save appearances, you protest
That you're betraying me at my behest.

MARIANE

Just as you say.

VALÈRE

Quite so. And I now see
That you were never truly in love with me.

MARIANE

Alas, you're free to think so if you choose.

VALÈRE

I choose to think so, and here's a bit of news:
You've spurned my hand, but I know where to turn
For kinder treatment, as you shall quickly learn.

MARIANE

I'm sure you do. Your noble qualities
Inspire affection . . .

[Act Two · Scene Four]

VALÈRE

                Forget my qualities, please.
They don't inspire you overmuch, I find.
But there's another lady I have in mind
Whose sweet and generous nature will not scorn
To compensate me for the loss I've borne.

MARIANE

I'm no great loss, and I'm sure that you'll transfer
Your heart quite painlessly from me to her.

VALÈRE

I'll do my best to take it in my stride.
The pain I feel at being cast aside
Time and forgetfulness may put an end to.
Or if I can't forget, I shall pretend to.
No self-respecting person is expected
To go on loving once he's been rejected.

MARIANE

Now, that's a fine, high-minded sentiment.

VALÈRE

One to which any sane man would assent.
Would you prefer it if I pined away
In hopeless passion till my dying day?

[*Act Two · Scene Four*]

Am I to yield you to a rival's arms
And not console myself with other charms?

MARIANE

Go then: console yourself; don't hesitate.
I wish you to; indeed, I cannot wait.

VALÈRE

You wish me to?

MARIANE

Yes.

VALÈRE

That's the final straw.
Madam, farewell. Your wish shall be my law.
(*He starts to leave, and then returns: this repeatedly:*)

MARIANE

Splendid.

VALÈRE (*Coming back again:*)

This breach, remember, is of your making;
It's you who've driven me to the step I'm taking.

[*Act Two · Scene Four*]

MARIANE

Of course.

VALÈRE (*Coming back again:*)

Remember, too, that I am merely
Following your example.

MARIANE

I see that clearly.

VALÈRE

Enough. I'll go and do your bidding, then.

MARIANE

Good.

VALÈRE (*Coming back again:*)

You shall never see my face again.

MARIANE

Excellent.

VALÈRE (*Walking to the door, then turning about:*)

Yes?

[*Act Two · Scene Four*]

MARIANE

What?

VALÈRE

What's that? What did you say?

MARIANE

Nothing. You're dreaming.

VALÈRE

Ah. Well, I'm on my way.
Farewell, *Madame.*
(*He moves slowly away.*)

MARIANE

Farewell.

DORINE (*To Mariane:*)

If you ask me,
Both of you are as mad as mad can be.
Do stop this nonsense, now. I've only let you
Squabble so long to see where it would get you.
Whoa there, Monsieure Valère!
(*She goes and seizes Valère by the arm; he makes a great show of resistance.*)

[Act Two · Scene Four]

VALÈRE

What's this, Dorine?

DORINE

Come here.

VALÈRE

No, no, my heart's too full of spleen.
Don't hold me back; her wish must be obeyed.

DORINE

Stop!

VALÈRE

It's too late now; my decision's made.

DORINE

Oh, pooh!

MARIANE (*Aside:*)

He hates the sight of me, that's plain.
I'll go, and so deliver him from pain.

[Act Two · Scene Four]

DORINE (*Leaving Valère, running after Mariane:*)

And now *you* run away! Come back.

MARIANE

No, no.
Nothing you say will keep me here. Let go!

VALÈRE (*Aside:*)

She cannot bear my presence, I perceive.
To spare her further torment, I shall leave.

DORINE (*Leaving Mariane, running after Valère:*)

Again! You'll not escape, Sir; don't you try it.
Come here, you two. Stop fussing, and be quiet.
 (*She takes Valère by the hand, then Mariane, and
 draws them together.*)

VALÈRE (*To Dorine:*)

What do you want of me?

MARIANE (*To Dorine:*)

What is the point of this?

DORINE

We're going to have a little armistice.

[Act Two · Scene Four]

(To Valère:)
Now, weren't you silly to get so overheated?

VALÈRE

Didn't you see how badly I was treated?

DORINE *(To Mariane:)*

Aren't you a simpleton, to have lost your head?

MARIANE

Didn't you hear the hateful things he said?

DORINE *(To Valère:)*

You're both great fools. Her sole desire, Valère,
Is to be yours in marriage. To that I'll swear.
      (To Mariane:)
He loves you only, and he wants no wife
But you, Mariane. On that I'll stake my life.

MARIANE *(To Valère:)*

Then why you advised me so, I cannot see.

VALÈRE *(To Mariane:)*

On such a question, why ask advice of *me?*

[*Act Two · Scene Four*]

DORINE

Oh, you're impossible. Give me your hands, you two.
(*To Valère:*)
Yours first.

VALÈRE (*Giving Dorine his hand:*)

But why?

DORINE (*To Mariane:*)

And now a hand from you.

MARIANE (*Also giving Dorine her hand:*)

What are you doing?

DORINE

There: a perfect fit.
You suit each other better than you'll admit.
(*Valère and Mariane hold hands for some time without looking at each other.*)

VALÈRE (*Turning toward Mariane:*)

Ah, come, don't be so haughty. Give a man
A look of kindness, won't you, Mariane?
(*Mariane turns toward Valère and smiles.*)

[*Act Two · Scene Four*]

DORINE

I tell you, lovers are completely mad!

VALÈRE (*To Mariane:*)

Now come, confess that you were very bad
To hurt my feelings as you did just now.
I have a just complaint, you must allow.

MARIANE

You must allow that you were most unpleasant...

DORINE

Let's table that discussion for the present;
Your father has a plan which must be stopped.

MARIANE

Advise us, then; what means must we adopt?

DORINE

We'll use all manner of means, and all at once.
        (*To Mariane:*)
Your father's addled; he's acting like a dunce.
Therefore you'd better humor the old fossil.
Pretend to yield to him, be sweet and docile,
And then postpone, as often as necessary,

[Act Two · Scene Four]

The day on which you have agreed to marry.
You'll thus gain time, and time will turn the trick.
Sometimes, for instance, you'll be taken sick,
And that will seem good reason for delay;
Or some bad omen will make you change the day—
You'll dream of muddy water, or you'll pass
A dead man's hearse, or break a looking-glass.
If all else fails, no man can marry you
Unless you take his ring and say "I do."
But now, let's separate. If they should find
Us talking here, our plot might be divined.
   (To Valère:)
Go to your friends, and tell them what's occurred,
And have them urge her father to keep his word.
Meanwhile, we'll stir her brother into action,
And get Elmire, as well, to join our faction.
Good-bye.

VALÈRE *(To Mariane:)*

  Though each of us will do his best,
It's your true heart on which my hopes shall rest.

MARIANE *(To Valère:)*

Regardless of what Father may decide,
None but Valère shall claim me as his bride.

VALÈRE

Oh, how those words content me! Come what will . . .

[*Act Two · Scene Four*]

DORINE

Oh, lovers, lovers! Their tongues are never still.
Be off, now.

VALÈRE (*Turning to go, then turning back:*)

One last word . . .

DORINE

No time to chat:
You leave by this door; and *you* leave by that.
(*Dorine pushes them, by the shoulders, toward opposing doors.*)

Act 3

SCENE ONE

DAMIS, DORINE

DAMIS

May lightning strike me even as I speak,
May all men call me cowardly and weak,
If any fear or scruple holds me back
From settling things, at once, with that great quack!

DORINE

Now, don't give way to violent emotion.
Your father's merely talked about this notion,
And words and deeds are far from being one.
Much that is talked about is left undone.

DAMIS

No, I must stop that scoundrel's machinations;
I'll go and tell him off; I'm out of patience.

DORINE

Do calm down and be practical. I had rather
My mistress dealt with him—and with your father.

[*Act Three · Scene One*]

She has some influence with Tartuffe, I've noted.
He hangs upon her words, seems most devoted,
And may, indeed, be smitten by her charm.
Pray Heaven it's true! 'Twould do our cause no harm.
She sent for him, just now, to sound him out
On this affair you're so incensed about;
She'll find out where he stands, and tell him, too,
What dreadful strife and trouble will ensue
If he lends countenance to your father's plan.
I couldn't get in to see him, but his man
Says that he's almost finished with his prayers.
Go, now. I'll catch him when he comes downstairs.

DAMIS

I want to hear this conference, and I will.

DORINE

No, they must be alone.

DAMIS

Oh, I'll keep still.

DORINE

Not you. I know your temper. You'd start a brawl,
And shout and stamp your foot and spoil it all.
Go on.

[Act Three · Scene One]

DAMIS

I won't; I have a perfect right . . .

DORINE

Lord, you're a nuisance! He's coming; get out of sight.
(*Damis conceals himself in a closet at the rear of the stage.*)

SCENE TWO

TARTUFFE, DORINE

TARTUFFE (*Observing Dorine, and calling to his manservant offstage:*)

Hang up my hair-shirt, put my scourge in place,
And pray, Laurent, for Heaven's perpetual grace.
I'm going to the prison now, to share
My last few coins with the poor wretches there.

DORINE (*Aside:*)

Dear God, what affectation! What a fake!

TARTUFFE

You wished to see me?

DORINE

Yes...

TARTUFFE (*Taking a handkerchief from his pocket:*)

For mercy's sake,
Please take this handkerchief, before you speak.

[Act Three · Scene Two]

DORINE

What?

TARTUFFE

Cover that bosom, girl. The flesh is weak,
And unclean thoughts are difficult to control.
Such sights as that can undermine the soul.

DORINE

Your soul, it seems, has very poor defenses,
And flesh makes quite an impact on your senses.
It's strange that you're so easily excited;
My own desires are not so soon ignited,
And if I saw you naked as a beast,
Not all your hide would tempt me in the least.

TARTUFFE

Girl, speak more modestly; unless you do,
I shall be forced to take my leave of you.

DORINE

Oh, no, it's I who must be on my way;
I've just one little message to convey.
Madame is coming down, and begs you, Sir,
To wait and have a word or two with her.

[*Act Three · Scene Two*]

TARTUFFE

Gladly.

DORINE (*Aside:*)

That had a softening effect!
I think my guess about him was correct.

TARTUFFE

Will she be long?

DORINE

No: that's her step I hear.
Ah, here she is, and I shall disappear.

SCENE THREE

ELMIRE, TARTUFFE

TARTUFFE

May Heaven, whose infinite goodness we adore,
Preserve your body and soul forevermore,
And bless your days, and answer thus the plea
Of one who is its humblest votary.

ELMIRE

I thank you for that pious wish. But please,
Do take a chair and let's be more at ease.
(They sit down.)

TARTUFFE

I trust that you are once more well and strong?

ELMIRE

Oh, yes: the fever didn't last for long.

[Act Three · Scene Three]

TARTUFFE

My prayers are too unworthy, I am sure,
To have gained from Heaven this most gracious cure;
But lately, Madam, my every supplication
Has had for object your recuperation.

ELMIRE

You shouldn't have troubled so. I don't deserve it.

TARTUFFE

Your health is priceless, Madam, and to preserve it
I'd gladly give my own, in all sincerity.

ELMIRE

Sir, you outdo us all in Christian charity.
You've been most kind. I count myself your debtor.

TARTUFFE

'Twas nothing, Madam. I long to serve you better.

ELMIRE

There's a private matter I'm anxious to discuss.
I'm glad there's no one here to hinder us.

[Act Three · Scene Three]

TARTUFFE

I too am glad; it floods my heart with bliss
To find myself alone with you like this.
For just this chance I've prayed with all my power—
But prayed in vain, until this happy hour.

ELMIRE

This won't take long, Sir, and I hope you'll be
Entirely frank and unconstrained with me.

TARTUFFE

Indeed, there's nothing I had rather do
Than bare my inmost heart and soul to you.
First, let me say that what remarks I've made
About the constant visits you are paid
Were prompted not by any mean emotion,
But rather by a pure and deep devotion,
A fervent zeal...

ELMIRE

No need for explanation.
Your sole concern, I'm sure, was my salvation.

TARTUFFE (*Taking Elmire's hand and pressing her fingertips:*)

Quite so; and such great fervor do I feel...

[Act Three · Scene Three]

ELMIRE

Ooh! Please! You're pinching!

TARTUFFE

'Twas from excess of zeal.
I never meant to cause you pain, I swear.
I'd rather...
(*He places his hand on Elmire's knee.*)

ELMIRE

What can your hand be doing there?

TARTUFFE

Feeling your gown; what soft, fine-woven stuff!

ELMIRE

Please, I'm extremely ticklish. That's enough.
(*She draws her chair away; Tartuffe pulls his after her.*)

TARTUFFE (*Fondling the lace collar of her gown:*)

My, my, what lovely lacework on your dress!
The workmanship's miraculous, no less.
I've not seen anything to equal it.

[Act Three · Scene Three]

ELMIRE

Yes, quite. But let's talk business for a bit.
They say my husband means to break his word
And give his daughter to you, Sir. Had you heard?

TARTUFFE

He did once mention it. But I confess
I dream of quite a different happiness.
It's elsewhere, Madam, that my eyes discern
The promise of that bliss for which I yearn.

ELMIRE

I see: you care for nothing here below.

TARTUFFE

Ah, well—my heart's not made of stone, you know.

ELMIRE

All your desires mount heavenward, I'm sure,
In scorn of all that's earthly and impure.

TARTUFFE

A love of heavenly beauty does not preclude
A proper love for earthly pulchritude;
Our senses are quite rightly captivated
By perfect works our Maker has created.

[*Act Three · Scene Three*]

Some glory clings to all that Heaven has made;
In you, all Heaven's marvels are displayed.
On that fair face, such beauties have been lavished,
The eyes are dazzled and the heart is ravished;
How could I look on you, O flawless creature,
And not adore the Author of all Nature,
Feeling a love both passionate and pure
For you, his triumph of self-portraiture?
At first, I trembled lest that love should be
A subtle snare that Hell had laid for me;
I vowed to flee the sight of you, eschewing
A rapture that might prove my soul's undoing;
But soon, fair being, I became aware
That my deep passion could be made to square
With rectitude, and with my bounden duty.
I thereupon surrendered to your beauty.
It is, I know, presumptuous on my part
To bring you this poor offering of my heart,
And it is not my merit, Heaven knows,
But your compassion on which my hopes repose.
You are my peace, my solace, my salvation;
On you depends my bliss—or desolation;
I bide your judgment and, as you think best,
I shall be either miserable or blest.

ELMIRE

Your declaration is most gallant, Sir,
But don't you think it's out of character?
You'd have done better to restrain your passion
And think before you spoke in such a fashion.
It ill becomes a pious man like you . . .

[Act Three · Scene Three]

TARTUFFE

I may be pious, but I'm human too:
With your celestial charms before his eyes,
A man has not the power to be wise.
I know such words sound strangely, coming from me,
But I'm no angel, nor was meant to be,
And if you blame my passion, you must needs
Reproach as well the charms on which it feeds.
Your loveliness I had no sooner seen
Than you became my soul's unrivalled queen;
Before your seraph glance, divinely sweet,
My heart's defenses crumbled in defeat,
And nothing fasting, prayer, or tears might do
Could stay my spirit from adoring you.
My eyes, my sighs have told you in the past
What now my lips make bold to say at last,
And if, in your great goodness, you will deign
To look upon your slave, and ease his pain,—
If, in compassion for my soul's distress,
You'll stoop to comfort my unworthiness,
I'll raise to you, in thanks for that sweet manna,
An endless hymn, an infinite hosanna.
With me, of course, there need be no anxiety,
No fear of scandal or of notoriety.
These young court gallants, whom all the ladies fancy,
Are vain in speech, in action rash and chancy;
When they succeed in love, the world soon knows it;
No favor's granted them but they disclose it
And by the looseness of their tongues profane
The very altar where their hearts have lain.

[*Act Three • Scene Three*]

Men of my sort, however, love discreetly,
And one may trust our reticence completely.
My keen concern for my good name insures
The absolute security of yours;
In short, I offer you, my dear Elmire,
Love without scandal, pleasure without fear.

ELMIRE

I've heard your well-turned speeches to the end,
And what you urge I clearly apprehend.
Aren't you afraid that I may take a notion
To tell my husband of your warm devotion,
And that, supposing he were duly told,
His feelings toward you might grow rather cold?

TARTUFFE

I know, dear lady, that your exceeding charity
Will lead your heart to pardon my temerity;
That you'll excuse my violent affection
As human weakness, human imperfection;
And that—O fairest!—you will bear in mind
That I'm but flesh and blood, and am not blind.

ELMIRE

Some women might do otherwise, perhaps,
But I shall be discreet about your lapse;
I'll tell my husband nothing of what's occurred
If, in return, you'll give your solemn word

[*Act Three · Scene Three*]

To advocate as forcefully as you can
The marriage of Valère and Mariane,
Renouncing all desire to dispossess
Another of his rightful happiness,
And . . .

SCENE FOUR

DAMIS, ELMIRE, TARTUFFE

DAMIS (*Emerging from the closet where he has been hiding:*)

No! We'll not hush up this vile affair;
I heard it all inside that closet there,
Where Heaven, in order to confound the pride
Of this great rascal, prompted me to hide.
Ah, now I have my long-awaited chance
To punish his deceit and arrogance,
And give my father clear and shocking proof
Of the black character of his dear Tartuffe.

ELMIRE

Ah no, Damis; I'll be content if he
Will study to deserve my leniency.
I've promised silence—don't make me break my word;
To make a scandal would be too absurd.
Good wives laugh off such trifles, and forget them;
Why should they tell their husbands, and upset them?

[Act Three · Scene Four]

DAMIS

You have your reasons for taking such a course,
And I have reasons, too, of equal force.
To spare him now would be insanely wrong.
I've swallowed my just wrath for far too long
And watched this insolent bigot bringing strife
And bitterness into our family life.
Too long he's meddled in my father's affairs,
Thwarting my marriage-hopes, and poor Valère's.
It's high time that my father was undeceived,
And now I've proof that can't be disbelieved—
Proof that was furnished me by Heaven above.
It's too good not to take advantage of.
This is my chance, and I deserve to lose it
If, for one moment, I hesitate to use it.

ELMIRE

Damis...

DAMIS

No, I must do what I think right.
Madam, my heart is bursting with delight,
And, say whatever you will, I'll not consent
To lose the sweet revenge on which I'm bent.
I'll settle matters without more ado;
And here, most opportunely, is my cue.

SCENE FIVE

ORGON, DAMIS, TARTUFFE, ELMIRE

DAMIS

Father, I'm glad you've joined us. Let us advise you
Of some fresh news which doubtless will surprise you.
You've just now been repaid with interest
For all your loving-kindness to our guest.
He's proved his warm and grateful feelings toward you;
It's with a pair of horns he would reward you.
Yes, I surprised him with your wife, and heard
His whole adulterous offer, every word.
She, with her all too gentle disposition,
Would not have told you of his proposition;
But I shall not make terms with brazen lechery,
And feel that not to tell you would be treachery.

ELMIRE

And I hold that one's husband's peace of mind
Should not be spoilt by tattle of this kind.
One's honor doesn't require it: to be proficient
In keeping men at bay is quite sufficient.
These are my sentiments, and I wish, Damis,
That you had heeded me and held your peace.

SCENE SIX

ORGON, DAMIS, TARTUFFE

ORGON

Can it be true, this dreadful thing I hear?

TARTUFFE

Yes, Brother, I'm a wicked man, I fear:
A wretched sinner, all depraved and twisted,
The greatest villain that has ever existed.
My life's one heap of crimes, which grows each minute;
There's naught but foulness and corruption in it;
And I perceive that Heaven, outraged by me,
Has chosen this occasion to mortify me.
Charge me with any deed you wish to name;
I'll not defend myself, but take the blame.
Believe what you are told, and drive Tartuffe
Like some base criminal from beneath your roof;
Yes, drive me hence, and with a parting curse:
I shan't protest, for I deserve far worse.

ORGON (*To Damis:*)

Ah, you deceitful boy, how dare you try
To stain his purity with so foul a lie?

[*Act Three · Scene Six*]

DAMIS

What! Are you taken in by such a bluff?
Did you not hear . . . ?

ORGON

Enough, you rogue, enough!

TARTUFFE

Ah, Brother, let him speak: you're being unjust.
Believe his story; the boy deserves your trust.
Why, after all, should you have faith in me?
How can you know what I might do, or be?
Is it on my good actions that you base
Your favor? Do you trust my pious face?
Ah, no, don't be deceived by hollow shows;
I'm far, alas, from being what men suppose;
Though the world takes me for a man of worth,
I'm truly the most worthless man on earth.
   (*To Damis:*)
Yes, my dear son, speak out now: call me the chief
Of sinners, a wretch, a murderer, a thief;
Load me with all the names men most abhor;
I'll not complain; I've earned them all, and more;
I'll kneel here while you pour them on my head
As a just punishment for the life I've led.

ORGON (*To Tartuffe:*)

This is too much, dear Brother.

[*Act Three · Scene Six*]
(*To Damis:*)
Have you no heart?

DAMIS

Are you so hoodwinked by this rascal's art . . . ?

ORGON

Be still, you monster.
(*To Tartuffe:*)
Brother, I pray you, rise.
(*To Damis:*)
Villain!

DAMIS

But . . .

ORGON

Silence!

DAMIS

Can't you realize . . . ?

ORGON

Just one word more, and I'll tear you limb from limb.

[Act Three · Scene Six]

TARTUFFE

In God's name, Brother, don't be harsh with him.
I'd rather far be tortured at the stake
Than see him bear one scratch for my poor sake.

ORGON (*To Damis:*)

Ingrate!

TARTUFFE

If I must beg you, on bended knee,
To pardon him . . .

ORGON (*Falling to his knees, addressing Tartuffe:*)

Such goodness cannot be!
(*To Damis:*)
Now, *there's* true charity!

DAMIS

What, you . . . ?

ORGON

Villain, be still!
I know your motives; I know you wish him ill:
Yes, all of you—wife, children, servants, all—
Conspire against him and desire his fall,

[Act Three · Scene Six]

Employing every shameful trick you can
To alienate me from this saintly man.
Ah, but the more you seek to drive him away,
The more I'll do to keep him. Without delay,
I'll spite this household and confound its pride
By giving him my daughter as his bride.

DAMIS

You're going to force her to accept his hand?

ORGON

Yes, and this very night, d'you understand?
I shall defy you all, and make it clear
That I'm the one who gives the orders here.
Come, wretch, kneel down and clasp his blessed feet,
And ask his pardon for your black deceit.

DAMIS

I ask that swindler's pardon? Why, I'd rather...

ORGON

So! You insult him, and defy your father!
A stick! A stick! (*To Tartuffe:*) No, no—release me, do.
   (*To Damis:*)
Out of my house this minute! Be off with you,
And never dare set foot in it again.

[*Act Three · Scene Six*]

DAMIS

Well, I shall go, but ...

ORGON

                Well, go quickly, then.
I disinherit you; an empty purse
Is all you'll get from me—except my curse!

SCENE SEVEN

ORGON, TARTUFFE

ORGON

How he blasphemed your goodness! What a son!

TARTUFFE

Forgive him, Lord, as I've already done.
             (*To Orgon:*)
You can't know how it hurts when someone tries
To blacken me in my dear Brother's eyes.

ORGON

Ahh!

TARTUFFE

    The mere thought of such ingratitude
Plunges my soul into so dark a mood ...
Such horror grips my heart ... I gasp for breath,
And cannot speak, and feel myself near death.

[*Act Three · Scene Seven*]

ORGON

(*He runs, in tears, to the door through which he has just driven his son.*)

You blackguard! Why did I spare you? Why did I not
Break you in little pieces on the spot?
Compose yourself, and don't be hurt, dear friend.

TARTUFFE

These scenes, these dreadful quarrels, have got to end.
I've much upset your household, and I perceive
That the best thing will be for me to leave.

ORGON

What are you saying!

TARTUFFE

They're all against me here:
They'd have you think me false and insincere.

ORGON

Ah, what of that? Have I ceased believing in you?

TARTUFFE

Their adverse talk will certainly continue,
And charges which you now repudiate
You may find credible at a later date.

[Act Three · Scene Seven]

ORGON

No, Brother, never.

TARTUFFE

Brother, a wife can sway
Her husband's mind in many a subtle way.

ORGON

No, no.

TARTUFFE

To leave at once is the solution;
Thus only can I end their persecution.

ORGON

No, no, I'll not allow it; you shall remain.

TARTUFFE

Ah, well; 'twill mean much martyrdom and pain,
But if you wish it . . .

ORGON

Ah!

[*Act Three · Scene Seven*]

TARTUFFE

                Enough; so be it.
But one thing must be settled, as I see it.
For your dear honor, and for our friendship's sake,
There's one precaution I feel bound to take.
I shall avoid your wife, and keep away . . .

ORGON

No, you shall not, whatever they may say.
It pleases me to vex them, and for spite
I'd have them see you with her day and night.
What's more, I'm going to drive them to despair
By making you my only son and heir;
This very day, I'll give to you alone
Clear deed and title to everything I own.
A dear, good friend and son-in-law-to-be
Is more than wife, or child, or kin to me.
Will you accept my offer, dearest son?

TARTUFFE

In all things, let the will of Heaven be done.

ORGON

Poor fellow! Come, we'll go draw up the deed.
Then let them burst with disappointed greed!

Act 4

SCENE ONE

CLÉANTE, TARTUFFE

CLÉANTE

Yes, all the town's discussing it, and truly,
Their comments do not flatter you unduly.
I'm glad we've met, Sir, and I'll give my view
Of this sad matter in a word or two.
As for who's guilty, that I shan't discuss;
Let's say it was Damis who caused the fuss;
Assuming, then, that you have been ill-used
By young Damis, and groundlessly accused,
Ought not a Christian to forgive, and ought
He not to stifle every vengeful thought?
Should you stand by and watch a father make
His only son an exile for your sake?
Again I tell you frankly, be advised:
The whole town, high and low, is scandalized;
This quarrel must be mended, and my advice is
Not to push matters to a further crisis.
No, sacrifice your wrath to God above,
And help Damis regain his father's love.

[Act Four · Scene One]

TARTUFFE

Alas, for my part I should take great joy
In doing so. I've nothing against the boy.
I pardon all, I harbor no resentment;
To serve him would afford me much contentment.
But Heaven's interest will not have it so:
If he comes back, then I shall have to go.
After his conduct—so extreme, so vicious—
Our further intercourse would look suspicious.
God knows what people would think! Why, they'd describe
My goodness to him as a sort of bribe;
They'd say that out of guilt I made pretense
Of loving-kindness and benevolence—
That, fearing my accuser's tongue, I strove
To buy his silence with a show of love.

CLÉANTE

Your reasoning is badly warped and stretched,
And these excuses, Sir, are most far-fetched.
Why put yourself in charge of Heaven's cause?
Does Heaven need our help to enforce its laws?
Leave vengeance to the Lord, Sir; while we live,
Our duty's not to punish, but forgive;
And what the Lord commands, we should obey
Without regard to what the world may say.
What! Shall the fear of being misunderstood
Prevent our doing what is right and good?
No, no; let's simply do what Heaven ordains,
And let no other thoughts perplex our brains.

[Act Four · Scene One]

TARTUFFE

Again, Sir, let me say that I've forgiven
Damis, and thus obeyed the laws of Heaven;
But I am not commanded by the Bible
To live with one who smears my name with libel.

CLÉANTE

Were you commanded, Sir, to indulge the whim
Of poor Orgon, and to encourage him
In suddenly transferring to your name
A large estate to which you have no claim?

TARTUFFE

'Twould never occur to those who know me best
To think I acted from self-interest.
The treasures of this world I quite despise;
Their specious glitter does not charm my eyes;
And if I have resigned myself to taking
The gift which my dear Brother insists on making,
I do so only, as he well understands,
Lest so much wealth fall into wicked hands,
Lest those to whom it might descend in time
Turn it to purposes of sin and crime,
And not, as I shall do, make use of it
For Heaven's glory and mankind's benefit.

CLÉANTE

Forget these trumped-up fears. Your argument
Is one the rightful heir might well resent;

[Act Four · Scene One]

It *is* a moral burden to inherit
Such wealth, but give Damis a chance to bear it.
And would it not be worse to be accused
Of swindling, than to see that wealth misused?
I'm shocked that you allowed Orgon to broach
This matter, and that you feel no self-reproach;
Does true religion teach that lawful heirs
May freely be deprived of what is theirs?
And if the Lord has told you in your heart
That you and young Damis must dwell apart,
Would it not be the decent thing to beat
A generous and honorable retreat,
Rather than let the son of the house be sent,
For your convenience, into banishment?
Sir, if you wish to prove the honesty
Of your intentions ...

TARTUFFE

Sir, it is half-past three.
I've certain pious duties to attend to,
And hope my prompt departure won't offend you.

CLÉANTE (*Alone:*)

Damn.

SCENE TWO

ELMIRE, MARIANE, CLÉANTE, DORINE

DORINE

Stay, Sir, and help Mariane, for Heaven's sake!
She's suffering so, I fear her heart will break.
Her father's plan to marry her off tonight
Has put the poor child in a desperate plight.
I hear him coming. Let's stand together, now,
And see if we can't change his mind, somehow,
About this match we all deplore and fear.

SCENE THREE

ORGON, ELMIRE, MARIANE, CLÉANTE, DORINE

ORGON

Hah! Glad to find you all assembled here.
              (*To Mariane:*)
This contract, child, contains your happiness,
And what it says I think your heart can guess.

MARIANE (*Falling to her knees:*)

Sir, by that Heaven which sees me here distressed,
And by whatever else can move your breast,
Do not employ a father's power, I pray you,
To crush my heart and force it to obey you,
Nor by your harsh commands oppress me so
That I'll begrudge the duty which I owe—
And do not so embitter and enslave me
That I shall hate the very life you gave me.
If my sweet hopes must perish, if you refuse
To give me to the one I've dared to choose,
Spare me at least—I beg you, I implore—
The pain of wedding one whom I abhor;
And do not, by a heartless use of force,
Drive me to contemplate some desperate course.

[Act Four · Scene Three]

ORGON (*Feeling himself touched by her:*)

Be firm, my soul. No human weakness, now.

MARIANE

I don't resent your love for him. Allow
Your heart free rein, Sir; give him your property,
And if that's not enough, take mine from me;
He's welcome to my money; take it, do,
But don't, I pray, include my person too.
Spare me, I beg you; and let me end the tale
Of my sad days behind a convent veil.

ORGON

A convent! Hah! When crossed in their amours,
All lovesick girls have the same thought as yours.
Get up! The more you loathe the man, and dread him,
The more ennobling it will be to wed him.
Marry Tartuffe, and mortify your flesh!
Enough; don't start that whimpering afresh.

DORINE

But why . . . ?

ORGON

      Be still, there. Speak when you're spoken to.
Not one more bit of impudence out of you.

[Act Four · Scene Three]

CLÉANTE

If I may offer a word of counsel here . . .

ORGON

Brother, in counseling you have no peer;
All your advice is forceful, sound, and clever;
I don't propose to follow it, however.

ELMIRE (*To Orgon:*)

I am amazed, and don't know what to say;
Your blindness simply takes my breath away.
You are indeed bewitched, to take no warning
From our account of what occurred this morning.

ORGON

Madam, I know a few plain facts, and one
Is that you're partial to my rascal son;
Hence, when he sought to make Tartuffe the victim
Of a base lie, you dared not contradict him.
Ah, but you underplayed your part, my pet;
You should have looked more angry, more upset.

ELMIRE

When men make overtures, must we reply
With righteous anger and a battle-cry?
Must we turn back their amorous advances
With sharp reproaches and with fiery glances?

[*Act Four · Scene Three*]

Myself, I find such offers merely amusing,
And make no scenes and fusses in refusing;
My taste is for good-natured rectitude,
And I dislike the savage sort of prude
Who guards her virtue with her teeth and claws,
And tears men's eyes out for the slightest cause:
The Lord preserve me from such honor as that,
Which bites and scratches like an alley-cat!
I've found that a polite and cool rebuff
Discourages a lover quite enough.

ORGON

I know the facts, and I shall not be shaken.

ELMIRE

I marvel at your power to be mistaken.
Would it, I wonder, carry weight with you
If I could *show* you that our tale was true?

ORGON

Show me?

ELMIRE

Yes.

ORGON

Rot.

[Act Four · Scene Three]

ELMIRE

          Come, what if I found a way
To make you see the facts as plain as day?

ORGON

Nonsense.

ELMIRE

       Do answer me; don't be absurd.
I'm not now asking you to trust our word.
Suppose that from some hiding-place in here
You learned the whole sad truth by eye and ear—
What would you say of your good friend, after that?

ORGON

Why, I'd say . . . nothing, by Jehoshaphat!
It can't be true.

ELMIRE

            You've been too long deceived,
And I'm quite tired of being disbelieved.
Come now: let's put my statements to the test,
And you shall see the truth made manifest.

ORGON

I'll take that challenge. Now do your uttermost.
We'll see how you make good your empty boast.

[*Act Four · Scene Three*]

ELMIRE (*To Dorine:*)

Send him to me.

DORINE

He's crafty; it may be hard
To catch the cunning scoundrel off his guard.

ELMIRE

No, amorous men are gullible. Their conceit
So blinds them that they're never hard to cheat.
Have him come down (*To Cléante & Mariane:*) Please
 leave us, for a bit.

SCENE FOUR

ELMIRE, ORGON

ELMIRE

Pull up this table, and get under it.

ORGON

What?

ELMIRE

It's essential that you be well-hidden.

ORGON

Why there?

ELMIRE

Oh, Heavens! Just do as you are bidden.
I have my plans; we'll soon see how they fare.
Under the table, now; and once you're there,
Take care that you are neither seen nor heard.

[Act Four · Scene Four]

ORGON

Well, I'll indulge you, since I gave my word
To see you through this infantile charade.

ELMIRE

Once it is over, you'll be glad we played.
   (*To her husband, who is now under the table:*)
I'm going to act quite strangely, now, and you
Must not be shocked at anything I do.
Whatever I may say, you must excuse
As part of that deceit I'm forced to use.
I shall employ sweet speeches in the task
Of making that imposter drop his mask;
I'll give encouragement to his bold desires,
And furnish fuel to his amorous fires.
Since it's for your sake, and for his destruction,
That I shall seem to yield to his seduction,
I'll gladly stop whenever you decide
That all your doubts are fully satisfied.
I'll count on you, as soon as you have seen
What sort of man he is, to intervene,
And not expose me to his odious lust
One moment longer than you feel you must.
Remember: you're to save me from my plight
Whenever . . . He's coming! Hush! Keep out of sight!

SCENE FIVE

TARTUFFE, ELMIRE, ORGON

TARTUFFE

You wish to have a word with me, I'm told.

ELMIRE

Yes. I've a little secret to unfold.
Before I speak, however, it would be wise
To close that door, and look about for spies.
    (Tartuffe goes to the door, closes it, and returns.)
The very last thing that must happen now
Is a repetition of this morning's row.
I've never been so badly caught off guard.
Oh, how I feared for you! You saw how hard
I tried to make that troublesome Damis
Control his dreadful temper, and hold his peace.
In my confusion, I didn't have the sense
Simply to contradict his evidence;
But as it happened, that was for the best,
And all has worked out in our interest.
This storm has only bettered your position;
My husband doesn't have the least suspicion,
And now, in mockery of those who do,
He bids me be continually with you.

[Act Four · Scene Five]

And that is why, quite fearless of reproof,
I now can be alone with my Tartuffe,
And why my heart—perhaps too quick to yield—
Feels free to let its passion be revealed.

TARTUFFE

Madam, your words confuse me. Not long ago,
You spoke in quite a different style, you know.

ELMIRE

Ah, Sir, if that refusal made you smart,
It's little that you know of woman's heart,
Or what that heart is trying to convey
When it resists in such a feeble way!
Always, at first, our modesty prevents
The frank avowal of tender sentiments;
However high the passion which inflames us,
Still, to confess its power somehow shames us.
Thus we reluct, at first, yet in a tone
Which tells you that our heart is overthrown,
That what our lips deny, our pulse confesses,
And that, in time, all noes will turn to yesses.
I fear my words are all too frank and free,
And a poor proof of woman's modesty;
But since I'm started, tell me, if you will—
Would I have tried to make Damis be still,
Would I have listened, calm and unoffended,
Until your lengthy offer of love was ended,
And been so very mild in my reaction,
Had your sweet words not given me satisfaction?

[Act Four · Scene Five]

And when I tried to force you to undo
The marriage-plans my husband has in view,
What did my urgent pleading signify
If not that I admired you, and that I
Deplored the thought that someone else might own
Part of a heart I wished for mine alone?

TARTUFFE

Madam, no happiness is so complete
As when, from lips we love, come words so sweet;
Their nectar floods my every sense, and drains
In honeyed rivulets through all my veins.
To please you is my joy, my only goal;
Your love is the restorer of my soul;
And yet I must beg leave, now, to confess
Some lingering doubts as to my happiness.
Might this not be a trick? Might not the catch
Be that you wish me to break off the match
With Mariane, and so have feigned to love me?
I shan't quite trust your fond opinion of me
Until the feelings you've expressed so sweetly
Are demonstrated somewhat more concretely,
And you have shown, by certain kind concessions,
That I may put my faith in your professions.

ELMIRE (*She coughs, to warn her husband.*)

Why be in such a hurry? Must my heart
Exhaust its bounty at the very start?
To make that sweet admission cost me dear,
But you'll not be content, it would appear,

[Act Four · Scene Five]

Unless my store of favors is disbursed
To the last farthing, and at the very first.

TARTUFFE

The less we merit, the less we dare to hope,
And with our doubts, mere words can never cope.
We trust no promised bliss till we receive it;
Not till a joy is ours can we believe it.
I, who so little merit your esteem,
Can't credit this fulfillment of my dream,
And shan't believe it, Madam, until I savor
Some palpable assurance of your favor.

ELMIRE

My, how tyrannical your love can be,
And how it flusters and perplexes me!
How furiously you take one's heart in hand,
And make your every wish a fierce command!
Come, must you hound and harry me to death?
Will you not give me time to catch my breath?
Can it be right to press me with such force,
Give me no quarter, show me no remorse,
And take advantage, by your stern insistence,
Of the fond feelings which weaken my resistance?

TARTUFFE

Well, if you look with favor upon my love,
Why, then, begrudge me some clear proof thereof?

[*Act Four · Scene Five*]

ELMIRE

But how can I consent without offense
To Heaven, toward which you feel such reverence?

TARTUFFE

If Heaven is all that holds you back, don't worry.
I can remove that hindrance in a hurry.
Nothing of that sort need obstruct our path.

ELMIRE

Must one not be afraid of Heaven's wrath?

TARTUFFE

Madam, forget such fears, and be my pupil,
And I shall teach you how to conquer scruple.
Some joys, it's true, are wrong in Heaven's eyes;
Yet Heaven is not averse to compromise;
There is a science, lately formulated,
Whereby one's conscience may be liberated,
And any wrongful act you care to mention
May be redeemed by purity of intention.
I'll teach you, Madam, the secrets of that science;
Meanwhile, just place on me your full reliance.
Assuage my keen desires, and feel no dread:
The sin, if any, shall be on my head.
         (*Elmire coughs, this time more loudly.*)
You've a bad cough.

[Act Four · Scene Five]

ELMIRE

Yes, yes. It's bad indeed.

TARTUFFE (*Producing a little paper bag:*)

A bit of licorice may be what you need.

ELMIRE

No, I've a stubborn cold, it seems. I'm sure it
Will take much more than licorice to cure it.

TARTUFFE

How aggravating.

ELMIRE

Oh, more than I can say.

TARTUFFE

If you're still troubled, think of things this way:
No one shall know our joys, save us alone,
And there's no evil till the act is known;
It's scandal, Madam, which makes it an offense,
And it's no sin to sin in confidence.

ELMIRE (*Having coughed once more:*)

Well, clearly I must do as you require,
And yield to your importunate desire.

[*Act Four · Scene Five*]

It is apparent, now, that nothing less
Will satisfy you, and so I acquiesce.
To go so far is much against my will;
I'm vexed that it should come to this; but still,
Since you are so determined on it, since you
Will not allow mere language to convince you,
And since you ask for concrete evidence, I
See nothing for it, now, but to comply.
If this is sinful, if I'm wrong to do it,
So much the worse for him who drove me to it.
The fault can surely not be charged to me.

TARTUFFE

Madam, the fault is mine, if fault there be,
And . . .

ELMIRE

  Open the door a little, and peek out;
I wouldn't want my husband poking about.

TARTUFFE

Why worry about the man? Each day he grows
More gullible; one can lead him by the nose.
To find us here would fill him with delight,
And if he saw the worst, he'd doubt his sight.

ELMIRE

Nevertheless, do step out for a minute
Into the hall, and see that no one's in it.

SCENE SIX

ORGON, ELMIRE

ORGON (*Coming out from under the table:*)

That man's a perfect monster, I must admit!
I'm simply stunned. I can't get over it.

ELMIRE

What, coming out so soon? How premature!
Get back in hiding, and wait until you're sure.
Stay till the end, and be convinced completely;
We mustn't stop till things are proved concretely.

ORGON

Hell never harbored anything so vicious!

ELMIRE

Tut, don't be hasty. Try to be judicious.
Wait, and be certain that there's no mistake.
No jumping to conclusions, for Heaven's sake!
   (*She places Orgon behind her, as Tartuffe re-enters.*)

SCENE SEVEN

TARTUFFE, ELMIRE, ORGON

TARTUFFE (*Not seeing Orgon:*)

Madam, all things have worked out to perfection;
I've given the neighboring rooms a full inspection;
No one's about; and now I may at last ...

ORGON (*Intercepting him:*)

Hold on, my passionate fellow, not so fast!
I should advise a little more restraint.
Well, so you thought you'd fool me, my dear saint!
How soon you wearied of the saintly life—
Wedding my daughter, and coveting my wife!
I've long suspected you, and had a feeling
That soon I'd catch you at your double-dealing.
Just now, you've given me evidence galore;
It's quite enough; I have no wish for more.

ELMIRE (*To Tartuffe:*)

I'm sorry to have treated you so slyly,
But circumstances forced me to be wily.

[Act Four · Scene Seven]

TARTUFFE

Brother, you can't think...

ORGON

                No more talk from you;
Just leave this household, without more ado.

TARTUFFE

What I intended...

ORGON

              That seems fairly clear.
Spare me your falsehoods and get out of here.

TARTUFFE

No, I'm the master, and you're the one to go!
This house belongs to me, I'll have you know,
And I shall show you that you can't hurt *me*
By this contemptible conspiracy,
That those who cross me know not what they do,
And that I've means to expose and punish you,
Avenge offended Heaven, and make you grieve
That ever you dared order me to leave.

SCENE EIGHT

ELMIRE, ORGON

ELMIRE

What was the point of all that angry chatter?

ORGON

Dear God, I'm worried. This is no laughing matter.

ELMIRE

How so?

ORGON

I fear I understood his drift.
I'm much disturbed about that deed of gift.

ELMIRE

You gave him . . . ?

[*Act Four · Scene Eight*]

ORGON

Yes, it's all been drawn and signed.
But one thing more is weighing on my mind.

ELMIRE

What's that?

ORGON

I'll tell you; but first let's see if there's
A certain strong-box in his room upstairs.

Act 5

SCENE ONE

ORGON, CLÉANTE

CLÉANTE

Where are you going so fast?

ORGON

God knows!

CLÉANTE

Then wait
Let's have a conference, and deliberate
On how this situation's to be met.

ORGON

That strong-box has me utterly upset;
This is the worst of many, many shocks.

CLÉANTE

Is there some fearful mystery in that box?

[Act Five · Scene One]

ORGON

My poor friend Argas brought that box to me
With his own hands, in utmost secrecy;
'Twas on the very morning of his flight.
It's full of papers which, if they came to light,
Would ruin him—or such is my impression.

CLÉANTE

Then why did you let it out of your possession?

ORGON

Those papers vexed my conscience, and it seemed best
To ask the counsel of my pious guest.
The cunning scoundrel got me to agree
To leave the strong-box in his custody,
So that, in case of an investigation,
I could employ a slight equivocation
And swear I didn't have it, and thereby,
At no expense to conscience, tell a lie.

CLÉANTE

It looks to me as if you're out on a limb.
Trusting him with that box, and offering him
That deed of gift, were actions of a kind
Which scarcely indicate a prudent mind.
With two such weapons, he has the upper hand,
And since you're vulnerable, as matters stand,
You erred once more in bringing him to bay.
You should have acted in some subtler way.

[Act Five · Scene One]

ORGON

Just think of it: behind that fervent face,
A heart so wicked, and a soul so base!
I took him in, a hungry beggar, and then . . .
Enough, by God! I'm through with pious men:
Henceforth I'll hate the whole false brotherhood,
And persecute them worse than Satan could.

CLÉANTE

Ah, there you go—extravagant as ever!
Why can you not be rational? You never
Manage to take the middle course, it seems,
But jump, instead, between absurd extremes.
You've recognized your recent grave mistake
In falling victim to a pious fake;
Now, to correct that error, must you embrace
An even greater error in its place,
And judge our worthy neighbors as a whole
By what you've learned of one corrupted soul?
Come, just because one rascal made you swallow
A show of zeal which turned out to be hollow,
Shall you conclude that all men are deceivers,
And that, today, there are no true believers?
Let atheists make that foolish inference;
Learn to distinguish virtue from pretense,
Be cautious in bestowing admiration,
And cultivate a sober moderation.
Don't humor fraud, but also don't asperse
True piety; the latter fault is worse,
And it is best to err, if err one must,
As you have done, upon the side of trust.

SCENE TWO

DAMIS, ORGON, CLÉANTE

DAMIS

Father, I hear that scoundrel's uttered threats
Against you; that he pridefully forgets
How, in his need, he was befriended by you,
And means to use your gifts to crucify you.

ORGON

It's true, my boy. I'm too distressed for tears

DAMIS

Leave it to me, Sir; let me trim his ears.
Faced with such insolence, we must not waver.
I shall rejoice in doing you the favor
Of cutting short his life, and your distress.

CLÉANTE

What a display of young hotheadedness!
Do learn to moderate your fits of rage.
In this just kingdom, this enlightened age,
One does not settle things by violence.

SCENE THREE

MADAME PERNELLE, MARIANE, ELMIRE, DORINE, DAMIS, ORGON, CLÉANTE

MADAME PERNELLE

I hear strange tales of very strange events.

ORGON

Yes, strange events which these two eyes beheld.
The man's ingratitude is unparalleled.
I save a wretched pauper from starvation,
House him, and treat him like a blood relation,
Shower him every day with my largesse,
Give him my daughter, and all that I possess;
And meanwhile the unconscionable knave
Tries to induce my wife to misbehave;
And not content with such extreme rascality,
Now threatens me with my own liberality,
And aims, by taking base advantage of
The gifts I gave him out of Christian love,
To drive me from my house, a ruined man,
And make me end a pauper, as he began.

DORINE

Poor fellow!

[Act Five · Scene Three]

MADAME PERNELLE

No, my son, I'll never bring
Myself to think him guilty of such a thing.

ORGON

How's that?

MADAME PERNELLE

The righteous always were maligned.

ORGON

Speak clearly, Mother. Say what's on your mind.

MADAME PERNELLE

I mean that I can smell a rat, my dear.
You know how everybody hates him, here.

ORGON

That has no bearing on the case at all.

MADAME PERNELLE

I told you a hundred times, when you were small,
That virtue in this world is hated ever;
Malicious men may die, but malice never.

[Act Five · Scene Three]

ORGON

No doubt that's true, but how does it apply?

MADAME PERNELLE

They've turned you against him by a clever lie.

ORGON

I've told you, I was there and saw it done.

MADAME PERNELLE

Ah, slanderers will stop at nothing, Son.

ORGON

Mother, I'll lose my temper... For the last time,
I tell you I was witness to the crime.

MADAME PERNELLE

The tongues of spite are busy night and noon,
And to their venom no man is immune.

ORGON

You're talking nonsense. Can't you realize
I saw it; saw it; saw it with my eyes?
Saw, do you understand me? Must I shout it
Into your ears before you'll cease to doubt it?

[*Act Five · Scene Three*]

MADAME PERNELLE

Appearances can deceive, my son. Dear me,
We cannot always judge by what we see.

ORGON

Drat! Drat!

MADAME PERNELLE

One often interprets things awry;
Good can seem evil to a suspicious eye.

ORGON

Was I to see his pawing at Elmire
As an act of charity?

MADAME PERNELLE

Till his guilt is clear,
A man deserves the benefit of the doubt.
You should have waited, to see how things turned out.

ORGON

Great God in Heaven, what more proof did I need?
Was I to sit there, watching, until he'd . . .
You drive me to the brink of impropriety.

[Act Five · Scene Three]

MADAME PERNELLE

No, no, a man of such surpassing piety
Could not do such a thing. You cannot shake me.
I don't believe it, and you shall not make me.

ORGON

You vex me so that, if you weren't my mother,
I'd say to you . . . some dreadful thing or other.

DORINE

It's your turn now, Sir, not to be listened to;
You'd not trust us, and now she won't trust you.

CLÉANTE

My friends, we're wasting time which should be spent
In facing up to our predicament.
I fear that scoundrel's threats weren't made in sport.

DAMIS

Do you think he'd have the nerve to go to court?

ELMIRE

I'm sure he won't: they'd find it all too crude
A case of swindling and ingratitude.

[*Act Five · Scene Three*]

CLÉANTE

Don't be too sure. He won't be at a loss
To give his claims a high and righteous gloss;
And clever rogues with far less valid cause
Have trapped their victims in a web of laws.
I say again that to antagonize
A man so strongly armed was most unwise.

ORGON

I know it; but the man's appalling cheek
Outraged me so, I couldn't control my pique.

CLÉANTE

I wish to Heaven that we could devise
Some truce between you, or some compromise.

ELMIRE

If I had known what cards he held, I'd not
Have roused his anger by my little plot.

ORGON (*To Dorine, as M. Loyal enters:*)

What is that fellow looking for? Who is he?
Go talk to him—and tell him that I'm busy.

SCENE FOUR

MONSIEUR LOYAL, MADAME PERNELLE, ORGON, DAMIS,
MARIANE, DORINE, ELMIRE, CLÉANTE

MONSIEUR LOYAL

Good day, dear sister. Kindly let me see
Your master.

DORINE

He's involved with company,
And cannot be disturbed just now, I fear.

MONSIEUR LOYAL

I hate to intrude; but what has brought me here
Will not disturb your master, in any event.
Indeed, my news will make him most content.

DORINE

Your name?

MONSIEUR LOYAL

Just say that I bring greetings from
Monsieur Tartuffe, on whose behalf I've come.

[Act Five · Scene Four]

DORINE (*To Orgon:*)

Sir, he's a very gracious man, and bears
A message from Tartuffe, which, he declares,
Will make you most content.

CLÉANTE

                    Upon my word,
I think this man had best be seen, and heard.

ORGON

Perhaps he has some settlement to suggest.
How shall I treat him? What manner would be best?

CLÉANTE

Control your anger, and if he should mention
Some fair adjustment, give him your full attention.

MONSIEUR LOYAL

Good health to you, good Sir. May Heaven confound
Your enemies, and may your joys abound.

ORGON (*Aside, to Cléante:*)

A gentle salutation: it confirms
My guess that he is here to offer terms.

[*Act Five · Scene Four*]

MONSIEUR LOYAL

I've always held your family most dear;
I served your father, Sir, for many a year.

ORGON

Sir, I must ask your pardon; to my shame,
I cannot now recall your face or name.

MONSIEUR LOYAL

Loyal's my name; I come from Normandy,
And I'm a bailiff, in all modesty.
For forty years, praise God, it's been my boast
To serve with honor in that vital post,
And I am here, Sir, if you will permit
The liberty, to serve you with this writ . .

ORGON

To—*what?*

MONSIEUR LOYAL

       Now, please, Sir, let us have no friction:
It's nothing but an order of eviction.
You are to move your goods and family out
And make way for new occupants, without
Deferment or delay, and give the keys . . .

[Act Five · Scene Four]

ORGON

I? Leave this house?

MONSIEUR LOYAL

Why yes, Sir, if you please.
This house, Sir, from the cellar to the roof,
Belongs now to the good Monsieur Tartuffe,
And he is lord and master of your estate
By virtue of a deed of present date,
Drawn in due form, with clearest legal phrasing . . .

DAMIS

Your insolence is utterly amazing!

MONSIEUR LOYAL

Young man, my business here is not with you,
But with your wise and temperate father, who,
Like every worthy citizen, stands in awe
Of justice, and would never obstruct the law.

ORGON

But . . .

MONSIEUR LOYAL

Not for a million, Sir, would you rebel
Against authority; I know that well.
You'll not make trouble, Sir, or interfere
With the execution of my duties here.

[Act Five · Scene Four]

DAMIS

Someone may execute a smart tattoo
On that black jacket of yours, before you're through.

MONSIEUR LOYAL

Sir, bid your son be silent. I'd much regret
Having to mention such a nasty threat
Of violence, in writing my report.

DORINE (*Aside:*)

This man Loyal's a most disloyal sort!

MONSIEUR LOYAL

I love all men of upright character,
And when I agreed to serve these papers, Sir,
It was your feelings that I had in mind.
I couldn't bear to see the case assigned
To someone else, who might esteem you less
And so subject you to unpleasantness.

ORGON

What's more unpleasant than telling a man to leave
His house and home?

MONSIEUR LOYAL

            You'd like a short reprieve?
If you desire it, Sir, I shall not press you,
But wait until tomorrow to dispossess you.

[*Act Five · Scene Four*]

Splendid. I'll come and spend the night here, then,
Most quietly, with half a score of men.
For form's sake, you might bring me, just before
You go to bed, the keys to the front door.
My men, I promise, will be on their best
Behavior, and will not disturb your rest.
But bright and early, Sir, you must be quick
And move out all your furniture, every stick:
The men I've chosen are both young and strong,
And with their help it shouldn't take you long.
In short, I'll make things pleasant and convenient,
And since I'm being so extremely lenient,
Please show me, Sir, a like consideration,
And give me your entire cooperation.

ORGON (*Aside:*)

I may be all but bankrupt, but I vow
I'd give a hundred louis, here and now,
Just for the pleasure of landing one good clout
Right on the end of that complacent snout.

CLÉANTE

Careful; don't make things worse.

DAMIS

                              My bootsole itches
To give that beggar a good kick in the breeches.

[*Act Five · Scene Four*]

DORINE

Monsieur Loyal, I'd love to hear the whack
Of a stout stick across your fine broad back.

MONSIEUR LOYAL

Take care: a woman too may go to jail if
She uses threatening language to a bailiff.

CLÉANTE

Enough, enough, Sir. This must not go on.
Give me that paper, please, and then begone.

MONSIEUR LOYAL

Well, *au revoir*. God give you all good cheer!

ORGON

May God confound you, and him who sent you here!

SCENE FIVE

ORGON, CLÉANTE, MARIANE, ELMIRE, MADAME PERNELLE, DORINE, DAMIS

ORGON

Now, Mother, was I right or not? This writ
Should change your notion of Tartuffe a bit.
Do you perceive his villainy at last?

MADAME PERNELLE

I'm thunderstruck. I'm utterly aghast.

DORINE

Oh, come, be fair. You mustn't take offense
At this new proof of his benevolence.
He's acting out of selfless love, I know.
Material things enslave the soul, and so
He kindly has arranged your liberation
From all that might endanger your salvation.

ORGON

Will you not ever hold your tongue, you dunce?

[*Act Five · Scene Five*]

CLÉANTE

Come, you must take some action, and at once.

ELMIRE

Go tell the world of the low trick he's tried.
The deed of gift is surely nullified
By such behavior, and public rage will not
Permit the wretch to carry out his plot.

SCENE SIX

VALÈRE, ORGON, CLÉANTE, ELMIRE, MARIANE, MADAME PERNELLE, DAMIS, DORINE

VALÈRE

Sir, though I hate to bring you more bad news,
Such is the danger that I cannot choose.
A friend who is extremely close to me
And knows my interest in your family
Has, for my sake, presumed to violate
The secrecy that's due to things of state,
And sends me word that you are in a plight
From which your one salvation lies in flight.
That scoundrel who's imposed upon you so
Denounced you to the King an hour ago
And, as supporting evidence, displayed
The strong-box of a certain renegade
Whose secret papers, so he testified,
You had disloyally agreed to hide.
I don't know just what charges may be pressed,
But there's a warrant out for your arrest;
Tartuffe has been instructed, furthermore,
To guide the arresting officer to your door.

[Act Five   Scene Six]

CLÉANTE

He's clearly done this to facilitate
His seizure of your house and your estate.

ORGON

That man, I must say, is a vicious beast!

VALÈRE

Quick, Sir; you mustn't tarry in the least.
My carriage is outside, to take you hence;
This thousand louis should cover all expense.
Let's lose no time, or you shall be undone;
The sole defense, in this case, is to run.
I shall go with you all the way, and place you
In a safe refuge to which they'll never trace you.

ORGON

Alas, dear boy, I wish that I could show you
My gratitude for everything I owe you.
But now is not the time; I pray the Lord
That I may live to give you your reward.
Farewell, my dears; be careful . . .

CLÉANTE

      Brother, hurry.
We shall take care of things; you needn't worry.

SCENE SEVEN

THE OFFICER, TARTUFFE, VALÈRE, ORGON, ELMIRE,
MARIANE, MADAME PERNELLE, DORINE, CLÉANTE, DAMIS

TARTUFFE

Gently, Sir, gently; stay right where you are.
No need for haste; your lodging isn't far.
You're off to prison, by order of the Prince.

ORGON

This is the crowning blow, you wretch; and since
It means my total ruin and defeat,
Your villainy is now at last complete.

TARTUFFE

You needn't try to provoke me; it's no use.
Those who serve Heaven must expect abuse.

CLÉANTE

You are indeed most patient, sweet, and blameless.

[Act Five · Scene Seven]

DORINE

How he exploits the name of Heaven! It's shameless.

TARTUFFE

Your taunts and mockeries are all for naught;
To do my duty is my only thought.

MARIANE

Your love of duty is most meritorious,
And what you've done is little short of glorious.

TARTUFFE

All deeds are glorious, Madam, which obey
The sovereign prince who sent me here today.

ORGON

I rescued you when you were destitute;
Have you forgotten that, you thankless brute?

TARTUFFE

No, no, I well remember everything;
But my first duty is to serve my King.
That obligation is so paramount
That other claims, beside it, do not count;

[Act Five · Scene Seven]

And for it I would sacrifice my wife,
My family, my friend, or my own life.

ELMIRE

Hypocrite!

DORINE

All that we most revere, he uses
To cloak his plots and camouflage his ruses.

CLÉANTE

If it is true that you are animated
By pure and loyal zeal, as you have stated,
Why was this zeal not roused until you'd sought
To make Orgon a cuckold, and been caught?
Why weren't you moved to give your evidence
Until your outraged host had driven you hence?
I shan't say that the gift of all his treasure
Ought to have damped your zeal in any measure;
But if he is a traitor, as you declare,
How could you condescend to be his heir?

TARTUFFE (*To the Officer:*)

Sir, spare me all this clamor; it's growing shrill.
Please carry out your orders, if you will.

[*Act Five · Scene Seven*]

OFFICER

Yes, I've delayed too long, Sir. Thank you kindly.
You're just the proper person to remind me.
Come, you are off to join the other boarders
In the King's prison, according to his orders.

TARTUFFE

Who? I, Sir?

OFFICER

Yes.

TARTUFFE

To prison? This can't be true!

OFFICER

I owe an explanation, but not to you.
         (*To Orgon:*)
Sir, all is well; rest easy, and be grateful.
We serve a Prince to whom all sham is hateful,
A Prince who sees into our inmost hearts,
And can't be fooled by any trickster's arts.
His royal soul, though generous and human,
Views all things with discernment and acumen;
His sovereign reason is not lightly swayed,
And all his judgments are discreetly weighed.

[*Act Five • Scene Seven*]

He honors righteous men of every kind,
And yet his zeal for virtue is not blind,
Nor does his love of piety numb his wits
And make him tolerant of hypocrites.
'Twas hardly likely that this man could cozen
A King who's foiled such liars by the dozen.
With one keen glance, the King perceived the whole
Perverseness and corruption of his soul,
And thus high Heaven's justice was displayed:
Betraying you, the rogue stood self-betrayed.
The King soon recognized Tartuffe as one
Notorious by another name, who'd done
So many vicious crimes that one could fill
Ten volumes with them, and be writing still.
But to be brief: our sovereign was appalled
By this man's treachery toward you, which he called
The last, worst villainy of a vile career,
And bade me follow the impostor here
To see how gross his impudence could be,
And force him to restore your property.
Your private papers, by the King's command,
I hereby seize and give into your hand.
The King, by royal order, invalidates
The deed which gave this rascal your estates,
And pardons, furthermore, your grave offense
In harboring an exile's documents.
By these decrees, our Prince rewards you for
Your loyal deeds in the late civil war,
And shows how heartfelt is his satisfaction
In recompensing any worthy action,
How much he prizes merit, and how he makes
More of men's virtues than of their mistakes.

[Act Five · Scene Seven]

DORINE

Heaven be praised!

MADAME PERNELLE

I breathe again, at last.

ELMIRE

We're safe.

MARIANE

I can't believe the danger's past.

ORGON (*To Tartuffe:*)

Well, traitor, now you see...

CLÉANTE

                       Ah, Brother, please,
Let's not descend to such indignities.
Leave the poor wretch to his unhappy fate,
And don't say anything to aggravate
His present woes; but rather hope that he
Will soon embrace an honest piety,
And mend his ways, and by a true repentance
Move our just King to moderate his sentence.
Meanwhile, go kneel before your sovereign's throne
And thank him for the mercies he has shown.

[*Act Five · Scene Seven*]

ORGON

Well said: let's go at once and, gladly kneeling,
Express the gratitude which all are feeling.
Then, when that first great duty has been done,
We'll turn with pleasure to a second one,
And give Valère, whose love has proven so true,
The wedded happiness which is his due.

BOOKS BY RICHARD WILBUR
AVAILABLE IN PAPERBACK EDITIONS FROM
HARCOURT BRACE JOVANOVICH, PUBLISHERS

Molière's The Misanthrope *and* Tartuffe *(translator)*

Molière's Tartuffe *(translator)*

The Poems of Richard Wilbur

Walking to Sleep: New Poems and Translations

Molière's The School for Wives *(translator)*

Responses

The Mind-Reader

Molière's The Learned Ladies *(translator)*

Opposites
(for children)

Racine's Andromache *(translator)*